WITHDRAWN

Books are to be returned on or before
the last date below.

7 – DAY
LOAN

23-10-02
5-31
28-10.02
2.28
28-10-02
4-30pm

LIBREX —

31 MAY 1994

D1422488

Theories of Imperialism

Theories of Imperialism

Wolfgang J. Mommsen

translated by P. S. Falla

Weidenfeld and Nicolson • *London*

German edition published under the title *Imperialismustheorien* © 1977 Vandenhoeck & Ruprecht, Göttingen
Translation copyright © 1980 George Weidenfeld and Nicolson Ltd and Random House, Inc.
First published in Great Britain in 1981 by
George Weidenfeld and Nicolson Ltd
91 Clapham High Street London SW4

ISBN 0 297 77794 7

Printed in Great Britain by
REDWOOD BURN LIMITED
Trowbridge & Esher

Preface

The present survey of recent theories of imperialism is the result of many years' study of problems connected with the interpretation of imperialism in modern times. It is based on a series of lectures given at Amsterdam University in 1970, and also owes much to the ideas of participants in many seminars and lecture courses at the University of Düsseldorf. A stay at St. Antony's College, Oxford, in 1971–72 enabled me to study at close quarters recent developments of British scholarship in this field. In conversation with Ronald Robinson at Balliol College I gained further information which helped me greatly to relate these new viewpoints to the present general study.

The review undertaken in this book has a limited purpose. Its first object is to provide a guide to the confusing medley of standpoints and opinions concerning the theory of imperialism. The critical analysis of the views described is a secondary purpose, and is expressly undertaken in particular cases only. At the present time there is a tendency for theoretical formulae concerning imperialism in general to be repeated without attention being paid to modern imperialism as a major historical phenomenon with a specific character of its own. In these circumstances it seems to me particularly important to bring out the historical dimension of the theory of imperialism. I also think it especially useful to reconcile the various socio-economic and political theories of imperialism with those which have for the first time directed attention emphatically to peripheral areas, whereas former theories were unduly Eurocentric.

To obtain a proper grasp of modern imperialism it is also necessary to take into account the various trends of Marxist-Leninist and Western neo-Marxist theories of the subject, even though it is precisely in this sphere that traditional formulae tend to be repeated like incantations—to the detriment of an analytical theory of imperialism, which should be more than a mere duplication of the theory of the capitalist world-system in its late capitalist phase. Neo-Marxist criticism singles out certain key problems of the present-day relationship between the industrialized countries and the third world, the solution of which is of great importance to the future of the West. This is the case irrespective of whether, like the neo-Marxist critics, we ascribe these problems to imperialism as such, or whether they are in fact structural problems of any industrial society and are unaffected by the difference between state and private ownership of the means of production or by the phenomenon of imperialist dependence, formal or informal as the case may be.

My thanks are due to Herr Hellmann of Vandenhoeck and Ruprecht for persistently urging me to complete the manuscript so that the book could be printed. I am also grateful to members of the history seminar at Düsseldorf University, who in many ways helped towards the completion of the work.

Wolfgang J. Mommsen
Düsseldorf, July 1976

Preface to the English Edition

This book was originally written with the intention of making a mainly German-speaking audience acquainted with the results of more recent research on the theories of imperialism, in particular in Great Britain. It discusses a wide range of theories developed since the turn of the century which still form the backbone of present-day thought on this subject, be it of the Marxist-Leninist, the Maoist or the neo-Marxist variety, or in the tradition of Western liberal thought. The book attempts to present a balanced picture of the various schools of thought on this issue, which is still a major element in the ideological struggle between the Marxist-Leninist camp and Western constitutional democracy. It is, moreover, an even graver cause of contention between the industrialised nations of the West, capitalist or otherwise, and the underdeveloped nations which are striving to overcome their backwardness, but which all too often have scarcely emerged from a struggle for mere survival.

One of the major objectives of this study has been to assign a proper place to the contribution made by English historians to the debate on the nature of imperialism, even though most of them have been reluctant to state their case in the systematic manner which has been predominant elsewhere. This is the case in particular with regard to the 'peripheral school,' which for the first time paid adequate attention to processes in the dependent territories and colonies on the periphery which had undoubtedly influenced the course of imperialist expansion a great deal. The presentation of the various theoretical positions is thus intended to serve as a kind of bridge between English and continental thought on the nature of imperialism. It may help to contribute to a better understanding of the various continental schools of thought, liberal, Marxist, objectivist or otherwise. Furthermore, there are substantial similarities in the approaches chosen by many recent British historians and the *dependencia* theoreticians, inasmuch as both emphasise the specific part played by the indigenous peoples, or at any rate, their élites, at the periphery. The theory of underdevelopment, however it may be evaluated from the academic point of view, certainly pinpoints one of the most critical present-day issues, namely the roots in the imperialist past of the uneasy and conflict-ridden relationship between the industrial nations of the West and the third world.

The author feels deeply indebted to the research achievements of many British and American writers on this subject whom it is impossible to enumerate here. It should perhaps be pointed out that the presentation of their views in the following pages is entirely the author's responsibility, and he can only hope that they will not find themselves treated in an unfair or one-sided manner. For all these reasons an English edition of this book is particularly welcomed by the author, and he wishes to express his sincere thanks to the publishers Weidenfeld & Nicolson and to Mr. P. S. Falla, who undertook the arduous task of rendering into readable English the often rather intricate reasoning of many of the theories discussed here, as well as the author's attempts to analyse these theories in a broader, comparative context.

w.j.m.

London, November 1979

Contents

Five Theories of Neo-Colonialism and Under-development

Six Summary and Prospects   142

Theories of Imperialism

one

Older Theories
of Imperialism

1 Classic political theories

Any consideration of early theories of imperialism must begin with the classic political interpretation that developed in the latter part of the nineteenth century and was brought into the domain of German scholarship by Heinrich Friedjung's *Das Zeitalter des Imperialismus 1884–1914*. [1] The original meaning of 'imperialism' was not the direct or indirect domination of colonial or dependent territories by a modern industrial state, but rather the personal sovereignty of a powerful ruler over numerous territories, whether in Europe or overseas. The Second Empire under Napoleon III ventured, it is true, on colonial experiments: these ended disastrously, but in any case they would hardly have enhanced the emperor's prestige or his actual power. Disraeli's famous Crystal Palace speech of 1872, announcing an ambitious programme of imperial expansion, was intended exclusively for home consumption: a forward overseas policy was proclaimed and pursued with the overt intention of enhancing the prestige of the Crown and strengthening the position of the Conservative Party. A final touch of splendour was conferred on this policy by Queen Victoria's assumption of the title Empress of India. It was Disraeli's opponents, especially Gladstone, who used the opprobrious term 'imperialism' to describe his policy of external aggression inspired by domestic motives.[2] Only in later years did the notion of imperialism acquire the comparatively objective meaning which it now bears. It lost the connotation of a system based on the pre-eminence of an imperial ruler and came to be generally understood as signifying the expansion of a nation state beyond its own borders for the purpose of acquiring overseas dependencies and if possible uniting them in a world-wide empire.

To Friedjung, who did most to introduce this classic political definition into the vocabulary of modern scholarship, imperialism signified both a nationalist ideology devoted to extending the domination of a particular nation state, and also a policy determined by ceaseless rivalry among the powers composing the international system of states. 'The spirit of restlessness was not content with developing the new or existing nation states. The peoples were seized with a new passion: they surged forth from their homelands to the ends of the earth, and devised the resounding name of "imperialism" for an urge that had always existed but had never been so powerful.'[3] Not only in Germany but in the rest of the Western world, imperialism was originally regarded as a phenomenon of power politics, consisting essentially in the extension of the rule of the European great powers to all parts of the globe. This was a purely political conception, addressing itself to the state as the decisive agent of history and attaching only secondary importance to the nationalist ways of thinking that were prevalent in ruling circles. From this point of view imperialism was the forcible extension of political rule to what were generally underdeveloped territories, regardless of the wishes of the conquered peoples. The object of acquiring a colonial empire was usually to enhance the prestige of one's own state, and ideally to raise it to the status of a world power.

Heinrich von Treitschke, for example, wrote before the turn of the century:

> Up to the present Germany has always had too small a share of the spoils in the partition of non-European territories among the powers of Europe, and yet our existence as a state of the first rank is vitally affected by the question whether we can become a power beyond the seas. If not, there remains the appalling prospect of England and Russia dividing the world between them, and in such a case it is hard to say whether the Russian knout or the English money-bags would be the more immoral and frightful alternative.[4]

In 1907 Otto Hintze put the same point more soberly but with no less conviction:

> The amount of energy devoted to economic and political affairs will determine which are to be the great powers of the future world system. The fight for great-power status is the true essence of the imperialist movement in the modern world. It is not a question, as in ancient times, of one power dominating the world, but of the selection of nations that are to take a leading part in world affairs.[5]

Similar ideas were expressed by contemporary British and French thinkers. Joseph Chamberlain and Paul Leroy-Beaulieu saw the imperialist expansion of the European great powers as an almost inevitable process: the world of the future would be dominated by great empires, and any nation state which did not join their ranks was condemned to inferior status. As Chamberlain put it in 1897: 'It seems to me that the tendency of the time is to throw all power into the hands of the greater empires, and the minor kingdoms—those which are non-progressive—seem to be destined to fall into a secondary and subordinate place.'[6]

In Germany before 1914 the same idea was expressed by Max Lenz and Erich Marcks in the theory of a necessary transition from the European political system to one of world states, a process in which Germany must join if it was not to become a second-class power.[7] It was Germany's historical mission to transform the European balance of power into a world equilibrium, even if this should involve a serious conflict with Great Britain. Similar voices were heard in the Anglo-Saxon countries: for example Sir John Seeley saw the expansion of England as largely a state responsibility devoted to creating a 'Greater Britain' and preserving for all time the unity of the British race. A kindred spirit in the United States was John William Burgess, who on the basis of a Hegelian concept of the state regarded it as inevitable that the US should become a world power.

This state-oriented theory of imperialism, conceived almost entirely in territorial terms, was closely allied to the idea of nationalism, since imperialism was generally regarded as a necessary consequence of the creation of nation states. The sources of the period provide a broad spectrum of nationalist arguments for imperial expansion. A vigorous policy of enlarging the territory of the nation state and creating an overseas empire—by force if necessary—was looked on by some as a necessary means of preserving and strengthening the national spirit, and by others as a source of fresh political vitality. Among German sources this viewpoint, which can already be traced among the early imperialists of the 1880s, was perhaps most trenchantly expressed by Max Weber in his inaugural address at Freiburg in 1894: 'We must realize that the unification of Germany was a youthful exploit performed by the nation in its old age, at so high a price that it should not have been undertaken if it was to be the end and not the beginning of a policy of turning Germany into a world power.'[8] Joseph Chamberlain, although he used chiefly economic arguments as to the necessity of imperial expansion or preserving and enlarging the British Empire, frequently referred to imperialism as an extension of nationalism. The nationalist variant of the political idea of imperialism was of extreme importance in legitimizing imperialist policies in all the major European countries. Investigation shows, however, that the formula of imperialism as a national necessity was extremely flexible and meant very different things in different cases. None the less, as we shall see, this idea is still highly influential at the present day. In 1931 Arthur Salz saw the idea of the nation as the 'strongest driving force of state imperialism'. Modern imperialism, in his view, did not rest on economic foundations but on supra-rational or rather emotional ones: what he called the 'new psychic structure of modern Europe', finding its supreme expression in modern nationalism.[9] In the same way, Walther Sulzbach endeavoured to explain the phenomenon of imperialism as an expression of nationalism.[10]

We must cast a brief glance at racial and biological variants of the concept of nationalist imperialism, which came increasingly to the fore in the later nineteenth century. According to this form of imperialism, peoples of the white race were inherently superior to those of other races and colours, and it was therefore their mission and duty to rule over them. This view found support in the theory of social Darwinism, according to which the struggle of different races for existence was a basic principle of history. Strong tendencies of this kind can be found in British and German imperialism before 1914: in England, for example, in the works of Benjamin Kidd and Karl Pearson, in Germany in those of Friedrich Naumann and, especially, Friedrich von Bernhardi and Houston Stewart Chamberlain.[11]

Today these racial and biological versions of imperialism may in general be looked upon as invalidated. Even if remnants of such ways of thinking still play a part in present-day politics, no one dares to espouse them openly. Imperialism of this particular type may be regarded as a thing of the past.

2 Classic economic theories

Not only the Marxists, but the theorists of the classic liberal capitalist economy were predominantly of the opinion that the possibilities of growth of the modern capitalist system were not unlimited and that it was therefore important, if not essential, to extend this system to virgin territories or, as they would today be called, the underdeveloped areas of the world. Considerations of this sort were already to be found in Hegel's *Philosophy of Right*. Accordingly we find it to be an almost constant element in bourgeois thought before 1914 that the capitalist economy needed overseas markets and investment opportunities and that it might be necessary to obtain them by imperialist means. The older liberal theory was that the spread of civilization, trade and industry all over the globe was a missionary activity and did not require the establishment of formal political sovereignty save in exceptional cases. For this reason many who believed in an economic order based on world trade and increased exports were for a long time opposed to imperialism in the narrower sense. They argued that, while imperialist policies enabled some firms to secure monopolistic profits at the expense of the community, they also distorted the process of economic growth in a way that was bound to have highly damaging consequences. It was only after a number of industrial states gradually went over to a protective tariff policy—Germany in 1879, France (with some of its colonies) in the 1890s and the United States around the turn of the century—that liberal circles began to take a more favourable view, on economic grounds, of territorial acquisitions overseas by their respective countries. Even so, while this view came to be widespread, we find no really systematic exposition of it in the bourgeois camp. Theodor Barth, for instance—an exponent of German left-wing liberalism before 1914—expressed the view that: 'Imperialism consists of influencing world economic processes, more or less violently, from the standpoint of the development of national power',[12] a formulation which betrays uncertainty as to whether he should be for imperialism or against it. In general there was much hesitation in the bourgeois camp as to whether formal imperialism was to be desired or whether informal economic expansion was sufficient; but there was relatively firm agreement that one of the principal objectives of modern imperialism was to provide national economies with fresh sources of raw materials, markets and profitable fields of investment overseas. These tendencies were related to the fact that from 1873 onwards the pace of international economic development began to slacken: there was a general fall in prices and a considerable diminution of profits. The conviction that national economies needed colonial dependencies soon became generally accepted by the bourgeois classes of all the industrial nations, and this was by no means merely the result of lobbying by the entrepreneurial groups directly concerned.

It is noteworthy, however, that these ideas were scarcely ever properly examined, but rather served as ideological counters in the argument for or against imperialism. The connection between economic interests and imperial expansion was as a rule taken for granted, and was only examined critically by opponents of imperialism. Among these were Charles A. Conant, an American who wrote for British radical journals, and especially J. A. Hobson. The latter produced shortly after the turn of the century a theory of modern imperialism which, though now out of date in almost all its details, is a classic of its kind and was extremely influential in its day.[13]

John Atkinson Hobson (1858–1940) was a publicist belonging to the left wing of the British Liberal Party, a consistent opponent of imperialism and advocate of an active social policy which would make Liberalism attractive to the working class. His interpretation of modern imperialism was based on his experience of the Boer War, which he witnessed at first hand as *Manchester Guardian* correspondent. His critique of British imperialism was in the tradition of English radicalism, which had always been sharply opposed to an aggressive foreign policy and was committed to the ideal of unrestricted free trade, not least on humanitarian grounds. In his book *Imperialism*, first published in 1902, Hobson denounced the jingoistic mood that prevailed in England at the outset of the Boer War, which he attributed mainly to unbridled propaganda by the press under the direction of capitalist interests. His chief aim was to preserve Liberalism from the effect of imperialist doctrine and pave the way for a consistent policy of social reforms. It is not accidental that the roots of his theory go back to studies of the problem of mass poverty in the great industrial cities of Britain.[14] With the aid of numerous statistics Hobson argued that the expansion of the Empire in recent decades was directly connected with the huge increase in British overseas investments. He inferred from this that the decisive factor making for imperialism was the endeavour of financial circles to find lucrative investment opportunities overseas in view of the saturation of the home market. The mainspring of imperialist policy was not so much the struggle for overseas markets as the search for profitable investments to compensate for diminishing returns at home. South Africa appeared to present a classic example of this. Hobson, it is true, by no means held that the capitalist system must in all circumstances give rise to imperialist policies. It was not capitalism as such, but the plutocratic structure of British society, denying the lower classes their rightful share of the national product, which engendered the evil of modern imperialism, with its enormous military and political cost and its inhuman consequences both at home and overseas. Because the working masses were allowed only an inadequate share of the national product, and the wealth of society was thus concentrated in the hands of a tiny upper class, there was on the one hand chronic 'oversaving', i.e., an excessive accumulation of capital seeking investment, and on the other 'underconsumption', i.e., insufficient demand on the home market. This led to a discrepancy between the economic potentiality of the capitalist system and the inadequate purchasing power of the masses; in consequence there was increasingly acute competition for profitable investments, and an inevitable decline in profits. Owners of capital were thus more and more drawn to invest abroad, especially in overseas colonial territories that had not yet been opened up economically: it was more profitable to look for opportunities there than to accept low returns from capital on the

home market. In order to take advantage of these opportunities the upper classes increasingly adopted a policy
of putting pressure on the government by stirring up
popular jingoism, so that political, diplomatic and if necessary military force might be used to acquire new overseas territories and open them up to capital investors,
especially those of one's own nation. In Hobson's view
the tremendous increase in British foreign investment,
and the breakneck pace at which African and Asian colonies were acquired or enlarged after 1880, were directly
linked to the relative economic stagnation and low standard of living of the working class in Britain itself. He
held that if the purchasing power of the masses could be
increased there would be sufficient opportunities of
profitable investment at home and the costly, and in the
last analysis unrewarding, policy of overseas expansion
by violent means would be unnecessary.

Hobson insisted that from the point of view of the
overall economic interest of society at large, imperialism
was not a source of profit but of loss. He criticized re-
morselessly the prevalent argument that British industry must have overseas outlets if it was to go on expanding. He illustrated by statistics what can probably now
be taken as proven, that Britain's trade with the colonies
acquired since 1870 was of only marginal importance
compared to her trade with the European industrial
countries. Nor was it true that the ratio of colonial to
European trade was increasing, as Joseph Chamberlain
and his followers were then arguing in support of their
demand for imperial preference. In any case the proceeds of trade with the undeveloped territories bore no
relation to the huge costs of armaments and administra-

tion involved in the creation and protection of a great overseas empire.

According to Hobson it was not the trader and entrepreneur but the investor, the capitalist in the true sense of the word, who was the prime mover, behind the scenes, of the great powers' struggle for colonies.

> Aggressive Imperialism, which costs the taxpayer so dear, which is of so little value to the manufacturer and trader, which is fraught with such grave incalculable peril to the citizen, is a source of great gain to the investor who cannot find at home the profitable use he seeks for his capital, and insists that his Government should help him to profitable and secure investments abroad.[15]

In other words, modern imperialism was due to the acute competition of surplus capital which did not find profitable employment on the home market.

This theory, which seemed self-evident in the case of the Boer War, was supported by certain key features of the British economic situation at the turn of the century. Interest rates at home were extremely low by modern standards, varying between 2 and 4 percent, while overseas the return on capital was considerably higher, though of course at a much greater risk. While the home economy showed clear signs of stagnation and the rise of real wages had come practically to a standstill, Britain's overseas investments were shooting up dramatically. In 1880 the total investment abroad was about £2 billion, while by 1913 it had risen to almost double this amount —a substantial proportion of the nation's capital.[16] Hobson interpreted this state of affairs in the light of Say's theory of underconsumption. Oversaving by the small upper class was matched by underconsumption on the part of the masses. This imbalance led to stagnation on the home market and a glut of capital seeking investment, with the evil consequence of imperialism which benefited only a small group of capitalists, whereas it was harmful to the nation as a whole and to its economic development.

To the question how it could be that broad sections of the population were carried away by nationalist enthusiasm for empire, even though imperialist policies were directly contrary to their own material interests, Hobson answered that this was due to manipulation of public opinion by the narrow circle of the ruling class which was directly interested in overseas investment. Using the popular press to whip up nationalist fervour, they were able to win over the masses to the idea of imperialism and hence induce them to support the narrow interests of capitalism. In this way Hobson's economic analysis of imperialism was supplemented by a socio-political analysis of mass behaviour, without which it was indeed not wholly convincing.

In general Hobson was not an opponent of capitalism as such, but rather a convinced free-trader who believed, with Adam Smith and Cobden, that industrial development on capitalist lines was in principle capable of bringing about a new and more humane world order. His conclusion was that 'It is not industrial progress that demands the opening up of new markets and areas of investment, but maldistribution of consuming power which prevents the absorption of commodities and capital within the country.'[17] With regard to this view, which is certainly oversimplified from the standpoint of

modern economic theory, especial note should be taken
of:

1. Hobson's opinion that, if the purchasing power of the
   masses was sufficiently increased, the home market would
   be capable of almost unlimited expansion, so that there
   was no need in principle of overseas outlets for capital;
2. his belief that the state could radically alter the character
   of the economic system by adjusting the distribution of
   the social product and thus increasing the masses' purchasing power.

Both these ideas were subsequently taken up by Keynes,
although in an essentially different way.

The conclusions Hobson drew from his analysis
were by no means radical. He urged that the disequilibrium within the economic system should be removed
by increasing the purchasing power of the masses,
chiefly by means of a broadly based social policy. This
would loosen the hierarchical structure of English society and raise the living standards of the population. Imperialism would soon be discarded by 'an intelligent
laissez-faire democracy which gave duly proportionate
weight in its policy to all economic interests alike'.[18]
For imperialism did not result from the principles of
capitalism as such, but from the anachronistic political
structure which enabled the upper classes to harness
the machinery of the state to their private interests and
manipulate the minds of the masses, exciting their
ambitions while keeping them at a low standard of
living that the state of economic development no
longer justified. The way to overcome imperialism
was not to do away with capitalism but to get rid of
the monopolistic structures that had come into being

in consequence of an anachronistic political order.

We may thus regard Hobson as a radical-liberal critic of imperialism, an adherent of the liberal views of Cobden and Adam Smith who wished, by restoring a fully competitive economy, to bring about the victory of a progressive form of radical liberalism. In his view imperialism was in the last resort a specific phenomenon of the transition from a politically anachronistic, capitalist society to an economically advanced social democracy: it was by no means a necessary product of capitalism as such. To the picture of imperialism as a movement fomented by groups of profit-greedy capitalists, he opposed the alternative of a free society of democratic peoples who, thanks to their national self-restraint in economic matters, were fitted to become members of a future world-wide federation of free nations.[19]

The repercussions of Hobson's theory of imperialism were varied and far-reaching. Most important is probably the fact that Lenin made extensive use of Hobson's data and arguments in his well-known work *Imperialism, the Highest Stage of Capitalism.* Hilferding, on the other hand, seems never to have noticed Hobson's views, although they were in fact closer to his own. The fact that Hobson's ideas are most strongly and directly reflected in Lenin's work has tended to obscure the fact that he had arrived at quite different conclusions: unlike the Marxists, Hobson believed that capitalism could be preserved by eliminating its predatory features. At the same time he did not believe that the future capitalist order could simply be left to the free interplay of forces, in orthodox liberal style: it must be constantly controlled by the state, under democratic supervision, in the interests of all classes, to the exclusion of one-sided privileges and positions of power.

Hobson's theory is impressive not only for the link it establishes between capital investment and imperialist policy, but especially for its analysis of the political milieu which enabled the upper class to impose its particular interests on society even though the masses, in principle at least, had the right to share in political decisions. His socio-psychological explanation of jingoism was later taken up by Hannah Arendt and developed in a broader context so as to link imperialism with fascism as mass movements, both of which came into being when, and in so far as, modern societies departed from the principle of a liberal, humanistic order. On the other hand it must be recognized that Hobson's direct correlation between capital export and colonial acquisitions is not borne out by statistical evidence. It is also accepted nowadays that banks were much less interested in imperial conquest than certain branches of industry. Again, Hobson did not fully prove his case that public opinion was effectively manipulated by capitalist interests. None the less he deserves credit for being the first to point out the link between imperialism and social structure on the one hand and economic factors on the other.

Professional economists have generally looked down on Hobson as an amateur whose theories took too little account of the differentiation of economic systems; but it is not accidental that Keynes, in particular, rediscovered his views and revived his theory of underconsumption despite its weaknesses. Perhaps Hobson's strongest influence on bourgeois theories of imperialism is to be found in Joseph Schumpeter's celebrated essay on 'The

Sociology of Imperialisms', first published in 1919 and consciously written as an answer to Marxist theories.[20] Hobson's view that the causes of imperialism lay primarily in the hierarchic structure of English society in the heyday of capitalism, and not in capitalism itself, can also be found in Schumpeter, as can the argument that the ruling classes, in order to defend their social position, fomented a jingoistic mood in which such ideas as national honour and prestige played an essential part.[21]

Before turning to Schumpeter, however, we should glance at the further development of theoretical conceptions of imperialism before 1914. Generally speaking these were not far-reaching. Little or no attempt was made during this period in bourgeois circles to analyse imperialism more thoroughly. Reference should, however, be made to Max Weber, since although he did not develop a consistent theory of imperialism, he did assemble important elements of such a theory from the sociological point of view.[22] Weber referred to the prestige aspect which led the great powers to engage in overseas expansion, and also pointed out that the ruling classes had a vested interest in imperialism because an extension of the national sovereignty normally increased their own social prestige and helped to buttress their privileged position and political prominence. 'Every successful imperialist policy of coercing the outside normally—or at least at first—also strengthens the domestic prestige and therewith the power and influence of those classes, status groups and parties under whose leadership the success has been attained.'[23] This predominantly sociological motive for imperial expansion was especially likely to appeal to ruling élites, and in Weber's view it was usually associated with specifically economic interests, particularly those of groups which sought monopoly profits instead of being content to manufacture and exchange goods in a formally free market. Monopolistic concessions of all kinds were especially likely to occur in the context of imperialist policy, and consequently financial groups and enterprises who were interested in this type of opportunity—among whom armament manufacturers were not the least important—could be relied on to support imperialist expansion. But Weber at the same time emphasized that this form of 'predatory capitalism' was as old as capitalism itself: it was in fact a parasitic form of genuine capitalism, considered as an economic system based on the production and rational exchange of goods within a market framework.

In addition Max Weber pointed to the specific interest of intellectuals in seeing the orbit of their national culture increased. This he regarded as a very important factor underlying the nationalist theory of imperialism, and one which was particularly influential with the bourgeoisie and the intelligentsia during the years before 1914:

It goes without saying that all those groups who hold the power to direct common conduct within a polity will be most strongly imbued with this idealist fervour of power prestige. They remain the specific and most reliable bearers of the idea of the state as an imperialist power structure demanding unqualified devotion.

In addition to the direct and material imperialist interests, discussed above, there are the indirectly material as well as the ideological interests of strata that are in various ways privileged within a polity and, indeed, privileged by its very existence. They comprise especially all those who think of themselves as being the specific 'partners' of a specific 'culture' diffused among the members of the polity.[24]

These observations of Weber's are of great importance, occupying as they do an intermediate position between the older political and the modern sociological theories of imperialism. They already contain all the elements of a systematic theory and were taken up in particular by Schumpeter, who however developed them in a very one-sided fashion.[25] Although Schumpeter's own views have often been sharply attacked on points of detail by more recent research, they form, as we shall see, an important source of modern Western theories.

Compared with Hobson's interpretation of imperialism, Schumpeter's rests on a much firmer theoretical basis; furthermore it is based upon a grandiose and comprehensive analysis of world history. At the same time, the two authors have much in common as regards their starting-point and ideological premises. Schumpeter, like Hobson, was a radical liberal with socialist tendencies, but was not attracted by the Marxist schema; again like Hobson, he was a firm adherent of the classical doctrine of free trade, and took as his guiding line the British model of a capitalist economy open to world-wide participation.

Schumpeter's analysis of imperialism, however, also took account of the Marxist analyses of Hilferding and Rosa Luxemburg, and endeavoured to present an alternative to them. He did so against the background of an impressively wide historical analysis of imperialist phenomena in all ages, with examples from the third millennium B.C. as well as the quite recent past. Schumpeter concluded that imperialism was not a product of capitalism but was a form of 'atavism' in the capitalist age, a survival from pre-industrial epochs and political structures.[26]

Schumpeter defined imperialism as 'the objectless disposition on the part of a state to unlimited forcible expansion'.[27] On this view imperialism is the result not of concrete economic interests or trends, but of the psychological attitude of aristocratic rulers: more precisely, it results from the warlike passions and inclinations which the ruling classes have in the course of history developed to a high degree and associated with social rewards. Not rational interests but ' "objectless" tendencies toward forcible expansion, without definite, utilitarian limits— that is, non-rational and irrational, purely instinctual inclinations towards war and conquest'—such was the real motivation of imperialism.[28] This thesis was supported by a wealth of historical examples, such as the Persian empire and ancient Rome, where the senatorial ruling class discovered that imperialism was the best way to keep the masses happy from a material and ideological point of view, or France under Louis XIV, where an idle aristocracy saw in war the true justification of its existence. Schumpeter regarded war and aggression as necessary elements in the preservation of feudal social structures—an argument well known to us in the shape of the current opinion concerning the war-producing tendency of Prussian militarism.

In short, Schumpeter attributed modern imperialism to the survival of residual political structures dating

from the time of absolute monarchy. Modern nationalism, too, derived in the last resort from the social tradi-
tions of militarism and absolutism. 'Nationalism is affir-
mative awareness of national character, together with an
aggressive sense of superiority.'[29]

Schumpeter regarded these traditional political structures as the direct opposite of modern liberal bourgeois
society. The latter was in principle cosmopolitan and
inclined to peaceful compromise within a system of un-
trammelled economic, cultural and intellectual exchange. In contrast to the survivals of older social structures that were still manifest in the warlike passions of
the masses and the nationalism of the great powers, capitalism in its modern industrial market-oriented form
represented a completely new social order which would
bring forth a new pacific type of man and would in
general reward quite different types of character. 'In a
purely capitalist world, what was once energy for war
becomes simply energy for labour of every kind.'[30] Para-
doxically, Schumpeter exalted the modern worker in
this context as a pacifist who was representative of the
new order and was vigorously opposed to imperialism
wherever it arose. From these socio-political premises
Schumpeter inferred that 'a purely capitalist world can
offer no fertile soil to imperialist impulses'.[31] Capitalism
was 'by nature anti-imperialist', and 'hence we cannot
readily derive from it such imperialist tendencies as actually exist, but must evidently see them only as alien
elements, carried into the world of capitalism from the
outside, supported by non-capitalist factors in modern
life'.[32]

It was quite wrong, therefore, to regard imperialism as

a favnt

the 'highest stage' of capitalism. It was rather an effect of the survival of older social structures within the developing capitalist system or, in other words, a transitional phenomenon pending the final triumph of capitalism. Schumpeter predicted that the future development of capitalism would not lead to an intensification of imperialism, but on the contrary would leave less and less room for imperialist policies. In principle he took the view that capitalism, at least in its pure form based on competition and a free market, was an alternative to all aristocratic forms of society and would put an end to all kinds of violent, 'objectless' expansion such as were inherent in them. It was therefore wrong to describe imperialism as a necessary phase of capitalism, or to think of capitalism as developing into imperialism. For the ways of the capitalist world were not such as to favour psychological attitudes of an imperialist kind, nor did the interests of the capitalist economy, or even its upper strata, point unequivocally in the direction of imperialist policy.[33]

Schumpeter conceded, however, that things were somewhat different in the conditions prevailing before 1914, when monopoly capitalism sought to control markets by means of artificial customs barriers, cartels and associations of all kinds, so that the principle of competition was to some extent prevented from operating. In conditions of monopoly capitalism, entrepreneurs and high finance might indeed find reasons to support imperialist policies. In Schumpeter's words:

> We have here, within a social group that carries great political weight, a strong, undeniable economic interest in such things as protective tariffs, cartels, monopoly prices, forced

exports (dumping), an aggressive economic policy, an aggressive foreign policy generally, and war, including wars of expansion with a typically imperialist character. Once this alignment of interests exists, an even stronger interest in a somewhat differently motivated expansion must be added, namely an interest in the conquest of lands producing raw materials and foodstuffs, with a view to facilitating self-sufficient warfare. Still another interest is that in rising wartime consumption. A mass of unorganized capitalists competing with one another may at best reap a trifling profit from such an eventuality, but organized capital is sure to profit hugely. Finally there is the political interest in war and international hatred which flows from the insecure position of the leading circles. They are small in numbers and highly unpopular. The essential nature of their policy is quite generally known, and most of the people find it unnatural and contemptible. An attack on all forms of property has revolutionary implications, but an attack on the privileged position of the cartel magnates may be politically rewarding, implying comparatively little risk and no threat to the existing order. Under certain circumstances it may serve to unite all the political parties. The existence of such a danger calls for diversionary tactics.[34]

Thus in a highly protectionist economy, capitalism, or more precisely the export of goods and capital, could definitely be 'aggressive' and a cause of imperialist actions and imperialist wars.

Schumpeter, however, regarded these phenomena as essentially due to political and social causes. He believed that monopolistic structures only came about when the political system specifically encouraged them—for example, by a policy of high tariffs; but this was the effect of an insufficient democratization of society, failing to keep pace with the development of the economic system.

Thus Schumpeter contrasted the monopoly capitalism of his own time with the ideal of a free system of autonomous entrepreneurs competing under a liberal democratic political regime. Monopoly capitalism was a departure from the true path, which was only possible because the capitalist class, influenced by survivals of pre-industrial social structures of an aristocratic type, was corrupted into monopolistic practices instead of allowing normal economic competition on a free market. A contributing cause was nationalist agitation by intellectuals in the service of the same reactionary groups. But Schumpeter was emphatically of the opinion that, in an age of advancing democracy, the overall trend was in the opposite direction, so that monopolistic structures were bound to disappear as the capitalist system became more democratic. Moreover, as the old-style ruling classes fell into the background, the 'combative instincts' that were still present in society would lose their importance and aggressive and warlike trends would gradually become a thing of the past.

The weaknesses of Schumpeter's theory of imperialism are today all too clear.[35] His alternative to the Marxist interpretation was based on the liberal pattern of a laissez-faire economy governed exclusively by the laws of a free market, in which there would be no monopolistic structures able to make use of the power of the state to further their private ends at the community's expense. One may feel that to evoke this picture in the conditions of 1918 was not only unjustified by the facts but was essentially the effect of an ideological *parti pris*. Nevertheless, Schumpeter's theory is a landmark in so far as he presented in ideal form the radical contrast between a liberal capitalist regime, in which economic activity and profits were subject to the laws of free-market competition, and imperialistic systems based on monopoly and exploitation. This was in line with the views of Max Weber, who had distinguished between normal capitalism, based on peaceful trading, and 'predatory capitalism', which was out to exploit monopolistic opportunities. Apart from this, however, it is questionable whether we can today be satisfied with Schumpeter's socio-psychological account of the behaviour of social groups, which is in some ways reminiscent of Freud. Schumpeter pays far less attention to the economic interests of particular groups than to the types of men or the systematic preference given within a certain social system to particular forms of human behaviour; it was the latter which in his opinion were the real determining factors of the historical process. Moreover he had no hesitation in drawing a sharp dividing line between free trade and imperialism; but this viewpoint is hard to maintain in the light of more recent research, as there was plenty of 'free-trade imperialism' in the first half of the nineteenth century. Many phenomena that Schumpeter classed as non-imperialistic would today be brought under the heading of 'free-trade imperialism', such as the economic expansionism of the United States in the twenty years before 1914.

None the less, Schumpeter's analysis of imperialism in the light of world history is an impressive achievement. Its particular merit was to draw attention to the typical behaviour patterns of specific groups in society, especially its ruling circles: in this respect he prepared the way for a modern sociological theory which would concentrate on showing how particular groups and classes within capitalist or non-capitalist systems were interested in imperialist expansion. From this point of view, although Schumpeter's theory is out of date in many respects, it is still an important point of departure for many recent interpretations of modern imperialism. This applies both to theories, such as those of Walt W. Rostow, which lay more stress on political factors interfering with capitalist developments, and to those which emphasize the imperialist tendencies displayed by ruling circles concerned to maintain their power during periods of rapid social change. These tendencies may continue to exist in tangible form in a social context in which the original, direct, material incentives have long ceased to operate.

two

Marxist Theories of Imperialism

1 Classic Marxist and Marxist-Leninist theories

The roots of Marxist theories of imperialism can all be found in their different variants in the writings of nineteenth-century bourgeois philosophers and political economists. The theory that the development of industrial capitalism must sooner or later come to a stop, thus bringing about a 'stationary state' in which there was no economic growth to speak of, was fairly widespread in the early nineteenth century: it can be found, for instance, in John Stuart Mill. It was often linked with the idea that the threat of stagnation could be at least temporarily averted by colonialism and imperialism. Repercussions of this line of thought are commoner than used to be supposed: for instance in Max Weber, who initially believed that the expansion of capitalism largely depended on the existence of economically 'free areas', and who consequently espoused an uncompromising imperialism:

Only complete political ignorance and naïve optimism can fail to see that the inevitable expansionist trade policy of the civilized bourgeois countries, having gone through a period of outwardly peaceful competition, is now quite certainly once again approaching the point at which only force can decide how far each of them is to share in the economic domination of the world, and consequently how much scope for economic betterment will be available to their population and especially the working class.[1]

Hegel, in his time, connected the phenomenon of colonialism with the division of bourgeois society into two classes (though the term itself was not yet used), 'when the standard of living of a large mass of people falls below a certain subsistence level—a level regulated automatically as the one necessary for a member of the society'.[2] The progress of industrialization brought, he argued, a polarization of society into a rabble and a small rich class. 'Despite an excess of wealth civil society is not rich enough, i.e., its own resources are insufficient, to check excessive poverty and the creation of a penurious rabble.'[3] 'This inner dialectic of civil society thus drives it—or at any rate drives a specific civil society—to push beyond its own limits and seek markets, and so its necessary means of subsistence, in other lands which are either deficient in the goods it has over-produced, or else generally backward in industry.'[4] Thus colonization is already presented here as a means of preventing or delaying the division of a society into two classes.

Curiously enough Karl Marx, who of course was thoroughly acquainted with Hegel's philosophical works, did not pick up this particular idea of his. Marx wrote in the age of free trade and the decline of old-style colonialism: his field of observation was early Victorian Britain, and he believed colonialism to be a specific phenomenon of early capitalism, the importance of which was diminishing. He only uses the term 'imperialism', in a sense quite different from the modern one, to denote the personal rule of Napoleon III. Marx held, in agreement with the bourgeois economists of his day, that the monopolistic practices of former colonialism were giving way to the all-powerful 'world market'. In *The German Ideology* he states that: 'In history up to the present it is certainly an empirical fact that separate individuals have, with the broadening of their activity into world-historical activity, become more and more enslaved under a power alien to them, . . . a power which has become more and more enormous and, in the last instance, turns out to be the world market.'[5] Marx, like the older economists, interpreted capitalism as essentially a closed system which could be reduced to certain general concepts whence its future development could logically be deduced. The world-wide expansion of industrial capitalism seemed to him both inevitable and objectively progressive. He noted without regret the destruction of outdated economic and social systems as a necessary stage towards bourgeois and eventually communist society. He approved of large economic areas and therefore implicitly of imperialism also, as an inevitable stage of world history which it was pointless to oppose. The extension of capitalism to hitherto undeveloped parts of the world seemed to him ultimately beneficial to humanity, however much human suffering it might cause. From a historical point of view, for instance, he regarded the British conquest of India as objectively progressive, since by it the methods of government and production associated with oriental despotism were eradicated and a basis laid for modern industry.[6] Only one theme—but an important one—of later Marxist theory concerning imperialism can be found in Marx himself, viz. the idea that external markets have a retarding and mitigating effect on economic crises. But Marx insisted that this, and imperialism in general, did not affect the basic validity of his predictions about the development of capitalism. On the contrary, he held that what went on in peripheral areas of the world was only of marginal importance to capitalism as a whole. The discovery of the revolutionary potential of backward countries, as seen in the relations between industrial states and undeveloped territories, is basically the work of later Marxism and Marxism-Leninism. In Marx's view the decisive processes were to take place in the centres of industrial development and not on the periphery.

With Friedrich Engels in the 1890s we find a shift of emphasis. Starting from the premise of a fundamental contradiction between the productive and the consumptive capacity of capitalist society, Engels was the first to address himself directly to the phenomenon of imperial expansion. The effect of the contradiction was that European powers expanded overseas in search of fresh markets. But Engels, too, regarded this state of things as purely transitional. External markets, in his view, had at first the effect of staving off crises but afterwards made them more acute, as they accelerated the increase of production and the concentration of capital. In other words,

Engels held firmly to the classic Marxist theory that capitalism would collapse at the end of a series of increasingly severe crises, and that imperialism, far from arresting this process, would in fact hasten it. In 1894 Engels remarked: 'Here is another splendid irony of history. China is the only country left for capitalist production to conquer, and once it does so it will have deprived itself of the possibility of surviving in its own home.'[7]

The idea of imperialism as an inevitable by-product of capitalism was developed by several socialist writers, for example, August Bebel, who in 1892 argued that production was far in excess of national needs, while the world was already carved up among the imperial nations, so that the collapse of capitalism was inevitable. The efforts of employers to depress workers' living standards still further meant that crises would perforce become more serious and widespread, as the workers' purchasing power continued to diminish. Bourgeois society would die of these inner contradictions.[8] Here again imperialism was still regarded as a marginal and inessential phenomenon; but the further events progressed, the harder it was for Marxists to ignore its central importance. The imperialism of the great European powers demanded a thorough explanation at a time when it was in the forefront of all political discussion, and when increasing expenditure on armaments and a rush to take possession of still unconquered territories were the order of the day.

At first the predominant tendency in the socialist camp was to regard imperialism as a direct continuation of colonialism, and as something of very doubtful merit even from the capitalist point of view. In particular, right-wing socialist critics of imperialism were close to the free-trade tradition which condemned it as bad for business. Kautsky, too, maintained that imperialism was 'not an economic necessity' but only 'one of many ways of promoting the extension of capitalism'.[9]

Among left-wing socialists, however, a view began to emerge according to which imperialism marked a new phase of the conflict between capitalist society and its opponents. This view rested on the premiss that there existed an organized proletarian movement, so that society was compelled to strengthen its means of political coercion more and more in order to defend itself against the growing power of the workers. The struggle for power beyond the national borders was only an aspect, or rather a means, of suppressing the proletarian movement. We find this idea especially in Rosa Luxemburg's early writings:

> If world politics have [this originally read 'China has'] become the scene of menacing conflicts, it is not so much a question of the opening up of new countries to capitalism. It is a question of already existing *European* antagonisms which, transported into other lands, have exploded there. The armed opponents we see today in Europe and other continents do not range themselves as capitalist countries on one side and backward countries on the other. They are states pushed to war especially as a result of their similarly advanced capitalist development.[10]

Imperialist expansion is thus primarily a reflection of the class struggle, which takes on more and more acute forms as capitalism develops towards its maturity. Nettl sums up this early view of Rosa Luxemburg's as follows: 'Imperialism above other things implied a totality, a

unity of action on the part of capitalist society, a sharp-
ening of its pressure on the socialists.'[11] The actual concept of 'imperialism' does not at first appear in this context at all: as far as the term is used, it is largely a synonym of 'militarism'. From the capitalists' point of view,
Rosa Luxemburg wrote as early as 1899:

> Militarism has become indispensable, first as a means of
> struggle for the defence of 'national' interests in competi-
> tion against other 'national' groups. Second, as a method of
> placement for financial and industrial capital. Third, as an
> instrument of class domination over the labouring popula-
> tion inside the country.[12] . . . Militarism, closely connected
> with colonialism, protectionism and power politics as a
> whole . . . a world armament race . . . colonial robbery and
> the policy of 'spheres of influence' all over the world . . . in
> home affairs the very essence of a capitalist policy of na-
> tional aggression.[13]

We have here not so much a theory in the strict sense,
but rather a kind of phenomenology of imperialism,
with strong polemical undertones and intended wholly
for purposes of political agitation. None the less, this
variant of the interpretation of imperialism has influenced Marxist-Leninist phraseology down to the present day. Imperialism is equated with reaction and the
repression of all liberation movements within the capitalist system, whether outside or inside the borders of a
given state. Militarism also plays a role as a substitute for
primary consumer capacity, since it constantly absorbs
part of the social product and thus makes economic
growth possible despite the increasing saturation of the
market.

A few years later Rosa Luxemburg embarked on a systematic theory of imperialism, to which we shall return.[14] The first genuinely Marxist theory of imperialism, however, came from Rudolf Hilferding, an Austrian Marxist who afterwards became a leader of the German Social Democratic Party and was finance minister in Hermann Müller's government in 1928–9. In 1910 he published *Das Finanzkapital*, a work which internal evidence shows to have been written in 1909; it provides a kind of reflection of the German economic landscape before 1914, with its multiplicity of cartels and industrial combinations.[15] In this work imperialism was first treated not as a marginal phenomenon but as a necessary accompaniment of capitalism at a stage of development beyond that of free trade. Hilferding's theory of imperialism presents itself as a contrast to Schumpeter's. Whereas the latter regards cartels, protectionism and monopoly capitalism as due primarily to political causes and in no way inherent in capitalism as such, Hilferding argues that monopoly capitalism and imperialism are a logical stage in the evolution of capitalism. He describes phenomena familiar to us, such as the emergence of large concerns, trusts and combines, protectionism, dumping and similar practices, all culminating in the predominance of banks or of 'finance capital'.

Hilferding concluded that capitalism under the domination of finance capital was diametrically opposed to laissez-faire capitalism in which individual entrepreneurs had competed against one another.

Finance capital seeks domination, not freedom: it has no interest in the independence of the individual capitalist, but requires his subjection. It abhors the anarchy of competition and demands organization, admittedly so that competition can be resumed at a higher level. But in order to achieve this, to maintain and increase its predominance, it needs the state to guarantee its home markets by customs and tariff policies and to conquer foreign markets. It needs a politically powerful state which can pursue its own commercial policy regardless of the conflicting interests of other states. Finally it needs a powerful state to assert its financial interests abroad and exert political pressure on smaller states to secure better terms of delivery and favourable commercial treaties. The state must be able to intervene anywhere in the world, so that the whole world can provide outlets for its finance capital. Altogether finance capital needs a state that is strong enough to pursue an expansionist policy and acquire new colonies.[16]

In Hilferding's view this expansionism was given ideological justification by a 'deflection of the national idea and racial ideology' in the direction of imperialism. He described this graphically in the following terms: 'The ideal nowadays is to make one's own nation master of the world—a limitless endeavour, as much so as the capitalist drive for profits from which it originates. Capital becomes the conqueror of the world, and with each new country it acquires a new frontier as a further jumping-off point.'[17] But all this, according to Hilferding, was also a matter of economic necessity, since 'any faltering of the onward drive reduces the profits of finance capital, weakens its powers of competition and finally turns the smaller economic area into a tributary of the larger'.[18] The thought adumbrated here was strongly to influence later discussions, especially concerning the increasing gap between the economic development of the industrial countries and those of the third world.

Hilferding, however, was not primarily interested in this problem: he held to the orthodox Marxist schema, although modifying it in important ways. He saw the situation as follows:

1. Imperialist expansion of all kinds (export of capital, gaining of external markets, opening up new territories, armaments policy, etc.) accelerates the expansion of capitalism.
2. In the expansionist phase capitalism is less vulnerable to crises. 'The more rapidly . . . capitalism expands, the longer is the period of prosperity and the shorter are the crises.'

This was an important variation of the theory of crises put forward by Marx and Engels. They had argued that the depressions which occurred every ten years would become increasingly severe until capitalism was bound to collapse; but the course of events down to 1914 had not borne out this prediction. From 1896 onwards there had in fact been a period of almost continuous economic growth and prosperity. Hilferding's explanation was that 'The opening up of the Far East and the rapid development of Canada, South Africa and South America are the chief reasons why capitalism has developed at such a dizzy rate since 1895, with only short periods of depression.' In the longer term, however, he predicted an opposite course of events. Periods of recession increased the power of finance capital and hence the danger of war. This increase in the power of finance capital was, according to Hilferding, the direct prelude to socialism:

Finance capital in its perfection denotes the highest stage of economic and political power in the hands of the capitalist oligarchy. It brings the dictatorship of the capital magnates to perfection. At the same time it means that the dictatorship of capitalists in one country is less and less compatible with the capitalist interests of another; while the domination of capital at home is more and more at variance with the interests of the masses who are exploited by finance capital but are also called on to fight. In the violent clash of hostile interests the dictatorship of capitalist magnates is transformed into the dictatorship of the proletariat.[19]

This is a powerful, coherent theory which, although dated in some respects, nevertheless contains important insights, including an exact prediction of the First World War. We shall not discuss for the present whether Hilferding's analysis of imperialism is universally valid: it must in any case be borne in mind that he had in view primarily the specific phenomenon of the industrialization of Germany. According to Gerschenkron and Sweezy,[20] his interpretation of imperialism as signifying the domination of finance capital applies specifically to a transitional phase in the development of the modern capitalist system, during which the banks played a special part as promoters of industrial development, but not to a fully matured capitalist economy as such.

A few years after Hilferding's work, in 1913, Rosa Luxemburg published *Die Akkumulation des Kapitals (The Accumulation of Capital)*. She regarded this work as a necessary supplement to Marx's theory of the development of modern capitalism: in contrast to her earlier writings, which for the most part dealt with the subject in an incidental and polemical fashion, she now set out to provide a general theory of imperialism. *The Accumulation of Capital* tackles the subject from the opposite point of view to her earlier works, already mentioned, in that it concentrates on the colonial dependencies of capitalist states. The weakness of her theory lies chiefly in her obstinate adherence to Marx's general schema of capital reproduction, as well as her reliance on a rather simplistic theory of underconsumption. In addition her argument was frequently dictated by considerations of political tactics which impaired its logical force.

Rosa Luxemburg began with the question why Marx's prediction of the inevitable collapse of capitalism had not yet come true. She claimed to have found the answer by means of a modification of Marx's theory of capital reproduction. Marx had described the development of capitalism, and especially the process of capital accumulation, within a 'closed system', overlooking the fact that the continued accumulation of capital presupposed the existence of areas which were not yet intensively exploited by capitalism, and could not take place without them. In other words, given the restriction of the purchasing power of the masses, the transformation of surplus value into investment capital could not be achieved without exploiting pre-capitalistic social structures:

From the very beginning, the forms and laws of capitalist production aim to comprise the entire globe as a store of productive forces. Capital, impelled to appropriate productive forces for purposes of exploitation, ransacks the whole world, it procures its means of production from all corners of the earth, seizing them, if necessary by force, from all levels of civilization and from all forms of society. The problem of the material elements of capitalist accumulation, far from being solved by the material form of the surplus value that has been produced, takes on quite a different aspect. It becomes necessary for capital progressively to dispose ever more fully of the whole globe, to acquire an unlimited choice of means of production, with regard to both quality and quantity, so as to find productive employment for the surplus value it has realized.[21]

Overseas markets were thus necessary not merely as outlets but in order to realize the otherwise surplus value of the capitalist production of the industrial countries.

Rosa Luxemburg inferred from this that, contrary to Marx's view, capitalism depended on economically virgin territories for its development, not only in the initial stages but even more so during its maturity. Otherwise the process of capital accumulation would never have attained its present enormous scale, and indeed it could not continue at all. In support of this argument, which must be regarded as highly problematical, Rosa Luxemburg contended that:

> Internal capitalist trade can at best realize only certain quantities of value contained in the national product: the constant capital that has been used up, the variable capital, and the consumed part of the surplus value. That part of the surplus value, however, which is earmarked for capitalization must be realized elsewhere.[22]

The realization of the whole of the surplus value therefore depended on non-capitalist producers and consumers as such. 'Thus the immediate and vital condition for capital and its accumulation is the existence of non-capitalist buyers of the surplus value, which is decisive to this extent for the problem of capitalist accumulation.'[23]

Rosa Luxemburg's basic adherence to Marx's complicated and controversial theory of surplus value, which by definition accrued to capitalists alone, prevented her from considering whether, if the consumer capacity of the masses were increased, internal markets might not afford suitable opportunities for the profitable investment of 'unconsumed', i.e., reinvestable, surplus value. She may have been additionally misled by the phenomenon of rapidly growing overseas investment which was in everybody's minds at the time. In any case the conclusion she drew was as surprising in the circumstances then prevailing as it is topical at the present day. She represents the underdeveloped countries as an essential component of the capitalist system and as a temporary means of rescue:

> As we have seen, capitalism in its full maturity also depends in all respects on non-capitalist strata and social organizations existing side by side with it. It is not merely a question of a market for the additional product . . . Capital needs the means of production and the labour power of the whole globe for untrammelled accumulation; it cannot manage without the natural resources and the labour power of all territories. Seeing that the overwhelming majority of resources and labour power is in fact still in the orbit of pre-capitalist production . . . capital must go all out to obtain ascendancy over these territories and social organizations.[24]

In other words, capitalism can only survive if it goes on continually expanding. But this process of growth is only possible as long as there are pre-capitalist societies and territories that can be conquered and brought into the economic sphere of influence of the capitalist colonial powers. 'The solution envisaged by Marx lies in the dialectical conflict that capitalism needs non-capitalist social organizations as the setting for its development, that it proceeds by assimilating the very conditions which alone can ensure its own existence.'[25] Once the 'free territories' have been exhausted, capitalism will have reached the final limit of its development and must collapse.

But this somewhat mechanistic conclusion does not play the part in Rosa Luxemburg's thinking that might be expected. Her political attitude was opposed to the orthodox Marxist line of German social democracy, which held that the bourgeois system would of necessity collapse of its own accord and thus quasi-automatically make way for the working class. Rosa Luxemburg's analysis of the development of capitalism in its imperialist phase led her to believe, on the contrary, that the objective conditions of the capitalist system in this period would lead to more and more violent conflicts among capitalists and the industrialized countries:

With the high development of the capitalist countries and their increasingly severe competition in acquiring non-capitalist areas, imperialism grows in lawlessness and violence, both in aggression against the non-capitalist world and in ever more serious conflicts among the competing capitalist countries. But the more violently, ruthlessly and thoroughly imperialism brings about the decline of non-capitalist civilizations, the more rapidly it cuts the very ground from under the feet of capitalist accumulation. Though imperialism is the historical method for prolonging the career of capitalism, it is also a sure means of bringing it to a swift conclusion. This is not to say that capitalist development must be actually driven to this extreme: the mere tendency towards imperialism of itself takes forms which make the final phase of capitalism a period of catastrophe.[26]

Rosa Luxemburg has in mind here the oppression and exploitation not only of the population of colonial territories but also, and especially, of the proletariat at home. In this context, without fully realizing the importance of the point she was making, she was the first to draw attention to the part played by militarism—the piling up of armaments, generally financed by indirect taxes—as a subsidiary means of capital accumulation. Defence expenditure acted as an additional method of realizing surplus value—an idea which has been adopted in various forms by later Marxist thinkers. Rosa Luxemburg, however, stressed the fact that the accumulation of capital was accelerated by the extension of the capitalist system at the expense of older social structures and also by the increasing oppression of the working class at home:

Capital increasingly employs militarism for implementing a foreign and colonial policy to get hold of the means of production and labour power of non-capitalist countries and societies. This same militarism works in a like manner in the capitalist countries to divert purchasing power away from the non-capitalist strata. The representatives of simple commodity production [sc. artisans etc.] and the working class are affected alike in this way. At their expense the accumulation of capital is raised to the highest power, by robbing the one of their productive forces and by depressing the other's standard of living.[27]

Thus Rosa Luxemburg not only predicts that the working class will be increasingly worse off, if only in relative terms, but also that the old middle class will be crushed out of existence. A more realistic prophecy, and one well suited to the last years before 1914, is the following gloomy passage:

> The more ruthlessly capital, by means of militarism, sets about the destruction of non-capitalist strata at home and in the outside world, the more it lowers the standard of living for the workers as a whole, the greater are the effects on the day-to-day history of capital accumulation on the world stage. It becomes a string of political and social disasters and convulsions, and under these conditions, punctuated by periodical economic catastrophes or crises, accumulation can go on no longer.
>
> But even before this natural economic impasse of capital's own creating is properly reached, it becomes a necessity for the international working class to revolt against the rule of capital.[28]

Rosa Luxemburg's theory of imperialism thus culminates in an appeal for revolutionary action by the working masses, above all the proletariat of the industrial countries, to shorten by violent means the death-agony of capitalism in its imperialist phase. This idea has had a strong influence on Marxism in the countries of the third world.

To sum up once again: Rosa Luxemburg saw imperialism as a phenomenon which offered capitalism a further chance of survival, albeit only for a time. In her view imperialism was a necessary consequence of the inherently expansionist character of capitalism, and was moreover a condition of the possibility of further capital accumulation by a small capitalist class. Strictly speaking it was only a new phase of capitalism. However, while the self-destructive mechanisms of the system could be kept in check as long as capitalism was expanding all over the globe, they were bound to prevail as soon as this process came to an end. 'Imperialism is the political expression of the accumulation of capital in its competitive struggle for what is still left of the non-capitalist regions of the world.'[29]

Rosa Luxemburg formulated this position still more cogently in her celebrated 'Junius pamphlet' of 1916, *The Crisis in German Social Democracy*, where she wrote:

> The capitalist desire for imperialist expansion, as the expression of its highest maturity in the last period of its life, has the economic tendency to change the whole world into capitalistically producing nations, to sweep away all superannuated, pre-capitalist methods of production and of society, to subjugate all the riches of the earth and all means of production to capital, to turn the labouring masses of the peoples of all zones into wage slaves. . . . This brutal triumphal procession of capitalism throughout the world, accompanied by all the means of force, of robbery and of infamy, has one bright aspect: it has created the premises for its own final overthrow, it has established the capitalist world rule upon which, alone, the socialist world revolution can follow.[30]

Contemporary socialist thinkers were disturbed by Rosa Luxemburg's thesis, according to which capitalism might apparently still have a long life before it, and particularly by the economic arguments on which her view was based. Otto Bauer, for instance, criticized her severely on this score.[31] Lenin, although he owed much to her theories of imperialism, made no mention of them whatever in his subsequent work. To this day her views are regarded with misgiving by Marxist authors, although they are extremely topical in the emphasis she attached to the strategic role of underdeveloped countries in the development of the capitalist system.

In one respect Lenin's theory of imperialism, to which we now turn, represented a kind of recession from Rosa Luxemburg's ideas: viz., in his re-emphasizing the inherent tendencies of industrial capitalism in the metropolitan countries.[32] Lenin's celebrated work *Imperialism, the Highest Stage of Capitalism* (originally *The Last Stage of Capitalism*),[33] written in Switzerland during the spring of 1916, was based largely on Hilferding and also Hobson; some influence on Bukharin's part must also be assumed,[34] and much use was made of the work of bourgeois economists. Lenin argued violently against Rosa Luxemburg's thesis that capitalism could not survive without colonial dependencies. None the less his view came close to hers inasmuch as he called imperialism a form of capitalism in its 'highest stage'; Rosa Luxemburg had spoken of 'its highest maturity in the last period of its life'. Although Lenin's pamphlet has been exalted to canonical status in the communist world, it is primarily a polemical document of limited theoretical importance, directed chiefly against social-chauvinistic tendencies within German social democracy, while at the same time addressing itself to the question why the revolution had not yet taken place in the most advanced industrial countries. Lenin described imperialism as a phase of temporary postponement of the revolution and also the death-agony of capitalism. Although the expressive title of his work was in effect borrowed from Rosa Luxemburg, his arguments chiefly followed Hilferding and Hobson. His thesis was that imperialism was the monopolistic stage of capitalism itself. Capitalism in this phase was bound to expand by every possible means, including the export of capital, economic penetration with political support of all kinds, forcible annexation and imperialist war. Lenin made no distinction between colonies in the strict sense and nominally independent 'semi-colonial' territories, as he called them, which were brought under the influence of the great industrial nations by direct or indirect methods of economic or political penetration.

Lenin enumerated five features which, according to him, were comprised in the definition of imperialism as the monopolistic phase of capitalism:

1. The concentration of production and capital has developed to such a high stage that it has created monopolies which play a decisive role in economic life;
2. The merging of bank capital with industrial capital, and the creation, on the basis of this 'finance capital', of a financial oligarchy;
3. The export of capital as distinguished from the export of commodities acquires exceptional importance;
4. The formation of international monopolist capitalist associations which share the world among themselves;
5. The territorial division of the whole world among the biggest capitalist powers is completed.[35]

Forced capital export to underdeveloped territories appears here, as in Hobson, as an outlet for surplus capital, but also as a means of checking the fall in profit rates.

Lenin pointed out, however, that in the long term this process exacerbated the situation instead of mitigating it: for the world-wide expansion of capitalism intensified competition, so that profit rates tended to fall even faster. The end of the process would in any case be the self-destruction of capitalism, probably by way of imperialist wars.

Lenin described imperialism as a phase of steadily increasing conflict within the capitalist camp itself. He pointed to the (first) world war as a direct product of this situation, and as the immediate prelude to the collapse of capitalism. Accordingly, 'Capitalism in its imperialist stage leads directly to the most comprehensive socialization of production; it, so to speak, drags the capitalists, against their will and consciousness, into some sort of a new social order, a transitional one from complete free competition to complete socialization.'[36] Lenin recognized, indeed, that monopoly capitalism might for a time bring about a certain increase in economic growth and thus stave off catastrophic class conflicts; he also conceded that imperialism furnished monopoly capitalism with extra profits, thanks to which it was able for a time to bribe the upper stratum of the working class and win it over to social chauvinism. 'Imperialism has the tendency to create privileged sections among the workers and to detach them from the broad masses of the proletariat.'[37] But in Lenin's opinion, which he shared with Rosa Luxemburg, this phase was coming to an end as the carve-up of overseas territories was completed. At the same time disputes within the capitalist camp were becoming more and more acute as the world was increasingly divided into a few rich states and a large number of poor states dependent on them. In this connection Lenin, following Hobson, spoke of the development of the 'usurer state' which lived increasingly on capital export and 'clipping coupons', i.e., rentiers drawing dividends.

Lenin did not dispute, however, that capitalism as such was still capable of further development. 'On the whole, capitalism is growing far more rapidly than before; but this growth is not only becoming more and more uneven in general, its unevenness also manifests itself, in particular, in the decay of the countries which are richest in capital.'[38] Altogether, from a purely economic point of view, he regarded imperialism as 'capitalism in transition or, more precisely, moribund capitalism'.[39] He laid more emphasis on the 'decay' in the capitalist camp than the unevenness of economic development, which latter was taken up and given special prominence by Stalin and neo-Marxist theoreticians. Lenin for his part expected an early collapse of the capitalist system.

This, of course, was a miscalculation, and it can be shown to have rested largely on the fact that Lenin overestimated the importance of certain features of the capitalist system of his day while underrating its inner flexibility: Otto Bauer, by contrast, had warned against false hopes as early as 1913.[40] It was indeed of great importance that Lenin shifted the emphasis of the battle against capitalism and imperialism on to the political plane: in this he differed from most other theoreticians except Rosa Luxemburg. At an early stage he saw the opportunity of an alliance with the colonial peoples of the third world, in contrast to Rosa Luxemburg, who at that time was arguing in numerous pamphlets that nationalism was a bourgeois ideology and no longer had any significance for the proletariat. The encouragement of third-world nationalism seemed to Lenin a first-class way to revolutionize the colonial systems, and therefore a promising weapon with which to combat capitalism. In Lenin's famous 'Decree on Peace' of 8 November 1917 the right of peoples to self-determination was expressly extended to colonial peoples and used as a revolutionary weapon against the capitalist world.

Admittedly Lenin's reasons for exploiting liberation movements among the colonial peoples were politico-strategic rather than theoretical. This appeared clearly in the draft 'Theses on National and Colonial Questions', which Lenin presented at the Second World Congress of the Comintern in 1920, and which argued eloquently for a close alliance between Soviet Russia and all nationalist and colonial liberation movements.

> The world political situation has now placed the dictatorship of the proletariat on the order of the day. World political developments are of necessity concentrated on a single focus—the struggle of the world bourgeoisie against the Soviet Russian Republic, around which are inevitably grouped, on the one hand, the Soviet movements of the advanced workers in all countries, and, on the other, all the national liberation movements in the colonies and among the oppressed nationalities, who are learning from bitter experience that their only salvation lies in the Soviet system's victory over world imperialism.[41]

In the same context Lenin spoke sharply against the 'falseness of bourgeois-democratic phrases' by which the spokesmen of finance capital and imperialism sought to gloss over the colonial and financial enslavement of a vast majority of the world's population by a small minority of the richest and most advanced capitalist countries. The Comintern Congress passed a resolution declaring that 'In the main, European capitalism derives its strength less from the European industrial countries than from its colonial possessions'.[42]

Lenin's strategy on this point was taken up and consistently developed by Stalin, who in April 1923 said in his address to the Twelfth Congress of the Russian Communist Party: 'Either we succeed in stirring up, in revolutionizing, the remote rear of imperialism—the colonial and semi-colonial countries of the East—and thereby hasten the fall of imperialism; or we fail to do so, and thereby strengthen imperialism and weaken the force of our movement.'[43] In this way, almost unintentionally, the centre of gravity of the Marxist-Leninist theory of imperialism and the future of the capitalist system shifted from the centre to the periphery. Thus Stalin wrote in 1924:

(a) The world is divided into two camps: the camp of a handful of civilized nations, which possess finance capital and exploit the vast majority of the population of the globe; and the camp of the oppressed and exploited peoples in the colonies and dependent countries, which constitute that majority.

(b) The colonies and the dependent countries, oppressed and exploited by finance capital, constitute a vast reserve and a very important source of strength for imperialism.

(c) The revolutionary struggle of the oppressed peoples in the dependent and colonial countries against imperialism is the only road that leads to their emancipation from oppression and exploitation.

(d) The most important colonial and dependent countries have already taken the path of the national liberation movement, which cannot but lead to the crisis of world capitalism.

(e) The interests of the proletarian movement in the developed countries and of the national liberation movement in the colonies call for the union of these two forms of the revolutionary movement into a common front against the common enemy, against imperialism.

(f) The victory of the working class in the developed countries and the liberation of the oppressed peoples from the yoke of imperialism are impossible without the formation and the consolidation of a common revolutionary front. . . .[44]

Thus an alliance with the national movements in the colonies was openly proclaimed with the object of overthrowing capitalism from the periphery, even when the national movements as such were bourgeois and not proletarian. This variant of the Marxist-Leninist conception of imperialism has had important consequences up to the present day, but it has meant that important aspects of Lenin's theory have been thrust into the background.

In the 1920s the Marxist theoreticians of the Soviet camp had to recognize that a certain stabilization of capitalism had taken place. They drew consolation, however, from the fact that it was in the course of losing its colonial basis. The doctrine that capitalism necessarily led to imperialism was now applied in reverse, so to speak: imperialism was declared to be out of date, with the implication that capitalism must be nearing its end also.

At the same time, and also not by chance, renewed emphasis was given to the political aspect, viz., that of wars being caused by the inner antagonisms of the capitalist system, while less stress was laid on purely economic factors of disturbance in the imperialist phase. Stalin said in 1924: 'The law of uneven development of the imperialist countries and of the inevitability of imperialist wars remains in force today more than ever before.'[45] Marxist-Leninist theory has held to this doctrine until the most recent past. Not until the Twentieth Congress of the Soviet Communist Party (CPSU) (1956) was the theory proclaimed of 'peaceful coexistence' between different social systems, with the implication that there was at least a possibility of long-term periods of peace: thus tacitly consigning to oblivion the old thesis that the continued existence of the capitalist system was bound to lead to more and more acute conflicts and wars.

From the mid-twenties onwards the level of Marxist-Leninist theories of imperialism clearly declined. Tom Kemp, himself arguing from a Marxist point of view, has shown in *Theories of Marxism*[46] that the deductions of Soviet ideologists suffered from being too much adapted to the tactical needs of the moment. The catastrophic misjudgment by the CPSU of the Fascist and Nazi movements was in no small degree a consequence of the ossified theory of imperialism prevalent in the later stages of Marxism-Leninism. The world communist movement was to pay a heavy price for having believed that fascism, being the ultimate stage of imperialist capitalism, would be immediately followed by the victory of the proletariat and was in a sense preparing the way for it, while the fascist seizure of power was a clear demonstration of the 'social fascists' treachery to the working class.

It must be recognized, on the other hand, that there were Marxist theoreticians in the socialist camp in the 1920s and 1930s who contributed substantially to the study of imperialism. The work of Eugen (Jenö) Varga is of particular importance;[47] but Varga, precisely because he departed from Lenin's views in some respects, was subjected to many attacks and his conclusions were not always accepted. Broadly speaking his interpretation followed Lenin's, but he pointed to a number of important modifications of the capitalist system which called unmistakably for some correction of the prevailing Marxist-Leninist analysis. He drew attention to the increase of state capitalist forms of economic organization which, he believed, temporarily improved the chances of capitalism surviving, although it remained inherently subject to periodical crises. The essence of state capitalism, he declared, was 'the attempt in some way to overcome the contradiction between private acquisition and production in course of being socialized, and to safeguard the interests of the bourgeoisie as a class, or of its dominant strata, *vis-à-vis* the private interests of individual capitalists whose sole interest is to make their monopoly profits as high as possible.'[48] The growing influence of the state on the economy made it possible, by state intervention, to avert temporarily the effect of certain immanent factors of crisis in the capitalist system; and it was also possible to mitigate the effects of economic crises, which as such were inherent elements of that system, by the artificial stimulation of demand. But Varga emphatically rejected the view advanced by Hilferding at the Kiel congress of the German Social Democratic Party (SPD) in 1927 that western economies were about to enter a qualitatively new phase of 'organized capitalism':[49] in principle he still maintained the view that capitalism in the present age was 'moribund', if not actually dead.

Thus, despite modifications of detail, Varga held firmly to the Stalinist thesis that the 'decline of capitalism' was continuing unabated, and that this was due in considerable measure to the 'anti-imperialist revolution' of the colonial peoples.[50] The world economic crisis of 1929 seemed fully to confirm his view, and he thought it scarcely possible that capitalism would recover from it in the long run. The slump would, he believed, accelerate the decay of capitalism, increase tension between all classes of capitalist society and lead to large-scale warfare.[51] In principle, therefore, Varga remained orthodox, while noting objectively several new features of the development of capitalism. In 1947—having meanwhile been obliged to perform 'self-criticism'—he expressed the view that 'the capitalist society of our day is the same capitalism that we knew at the beginning of the century, and its inherent laws are the same now as they were then'.[52]

However, the Stalinist interpretation of Marxism-Leninism, according to which the break-up of the colonial empires would eventually deal a death-blow to capitalism, proved to be erroneous. Events after 1945 showed it to be no longer tenable, and it was logical to return to Lenin's interpretation which laid stress on the monopolistic character of capitalism. The theory of 'state monopoly capitalism' may be regarded as a continuation of the classical Leninist theory under the conditions of the period of decolonization. The main emphasis was now laid on the increased activity of the state in economic affairs and particularly in the role of militarism: these two factors were made to compensate for the clearly diminishing importance of colonial territories in the further development of capitalism. State monopolies and militarism were seen by orthodox Marxist-Leninists as clear symptoms of the advanced decay of the capitalist system.

Yet the Marxist-Leninists were by no means prepared to give up the use of the term 'imperialism' as a description of the relations between industrial and underdeveloped countries. Instead, the Stalinist conception of imperialism was developed into the theory that, since the Second World War, previous forms of direct, brutal, imperialist domination had been replaced by subtler forms of purely economic and technological control together with 'political influence', but that the real situation was exactly as before. There are numerous examples of this attitude, which serves far-reaching politico-strategic aims but has little to do with an objective analysis of the complicated problems involved. We may instance a working paper used at the Moscow Conference of Communist Parties in May 1969, as reported in the *Frankfurter Allgemeine Zeitung* of 31 May of that year, which read in part: 'Imperialism imposes economic treaties and military pacts on countries which limit their sovereignty; it exploits them by means of capital export, unequal trade relations, manipulation of prices and exchange rates, credits and various forms of so-called aid.'

Such uses of the word 'imperialism' increasingly deprive it of all precision and make it a mere synonym of 'capitalism'. Any political or economic action by Western states is branded as imperialist, regardless of whether international finance capital operates in Western industrial countries themselves or in underdeveloped regions of the world. Clearly the scientific value of such an approach is very slight. Arguments of this kind, however, are increasingly popular in third-world countries, where they afford a useful ideological weapon in aid of the national liberation movements of Africa and Asia.

2 Maoist variants of the Marxist-Leninist theory

Since the 1930s current official versions of Marxism-Leninism have been confronted by a serious rival in the shape of the Maoist theory of imperialism. This theory has had, and continues to have, considerable influence on the development of Marxist teaching in areas of the world which are not controlled, directly or indirectly, by the Soviet Union.

Maoism, in contrast to Leninism, has always laid stress on practice as opposed to theory, and from the theoretical point of view its ideas are not particularly elaborate. Maoist doctrine originally followed the lines laid down by Lenin and Stalin, its exposition of them being narrowly exact but also superficial. Most authors remark on its lack of originality compared with Marxism-Leninism, and some, such as Wittfogel, deny that there is such a thing as an independent Maoist doctrine.[53] It is indeed difficult to derive a systematic conception of imperialism from statements by Mao Tse-tung or other leading Chinese communist theoreticians, especially as they

are in general only available to us in selective form.
Basically Mao Tse-tung followed Lenin's and Stalin's
formulae, as for instance in his essay of 1937 'On Contradictions':

> When the capitalism of the era of free competition devel-
> oped into imperialism, there was no change in the class
> nature of the two classes in fundamental contradiction,
> namely the proletariat and the bourgeoisie, or in the capital-
> ist essence of society. However, the contradiction between
> these two classes became intensified, the contradiction be-
> tween monopoly and non-monopoly capitalism emerged,
> the contradiction between the colonial powers and the colo-
> nies became intensified, the contradiction among the capi-
> talist countries resulting from their uneven development
> manifested itself with particular sharpness, and thus there
> arose the special stage of capitalism, the stage of imperial-
> ism. Leninism is the Marxism of the era of imperialism and
> proletarian revolution, precisely because Lenin and Stalin
> have correctly explained these contradictions and correctly
> formulated the theory and tactics of the proletarian revolu-
> tion for solving them.[54]

This passage reproduces with fair precision what was
then the current version of the Marxist position, and in
all essential points it refers directly to Lenin. Only the
mention of increasing contradictions between the imperial powers and their colonies may be taken as reflecting
more strongly the special position of the Chinese com-
munists.

The starting-point of Maoism was thus more or less
the same as that of Marxism-Leninism, but subsequently
there was a distinct change of emphasis. While the official doctrine of the Eastern bloc cautiously toned down

the thesis that imperialism must lead to war under all circumstances, this continued to be an essential tenet of Maoism. Being born of war communism, Maoism had at all times something essentially militant about it, and this became a clear feature of its ideology. War, as a means of liberating the working class, was regarded by Maoists as the norm, whereas, in the area where orthodox communism held sway, it was considered as an exception or as a by-product of revolutionary upheaval. Compared with official Russian doctrine, the Chinese laid far more emphasis on the direct connection between the victory of communism in China and the victory of the underdeveloped countries over their imperialist masters. In 1935, during the 'fight against Japanese imperialism', Mao declared that:

> Ever since that monster imperialism came into being, things in the world have been organically connected with one another, and it is impossible to attempt to separate them. We Chinese people possess the heroic spirit to wage the bloody war against the enemies to the finish, the determination to recover our lost territory through our own efforts, and the ability to stand on our own feet in the family of nations of the world. But this does not mean that we can dispense with international support; no, international support is necessary for the revolutionary struggle today in any country or of any nation. As the ancients put it, 'There were no just wars in the Era of Spring and Autumn' [a quotation from Mencius, referring to a period of feudal strife]. This is even more true of imperialism today, and it is only the oppressed nations and the oppressed classes that can wage just wars. All those wars in the world in which the people rise to fight their oppressors are just wars. . . . All just wars should support each other and all unjust wars should be turned into just ones.[55]

The Maoist variant of the Marxist-Leninist theory of imperialism is based first and foremost on this conception of a 'just war' against oppression by the capitalist powers. Only by way of mass revolt and open war against the imperialists could communism be victorious, according to the Maoist view, and the countries of the third world were increasingly assigned a leading role in this process. A leading article in the *Peking Review* of 8 October 1963, approved by Mao himself, acclaimed the liberation movements of the colonial peoples of Asia, Africa and Latin America:

> This mighty revolutionary storm makes the imperialists and colonialists tremble and the revolutionary people of the world rejoice. . . . Today the national-liberation revolutions in Asia, Africa and Latin America are the most important forces dealing imperialism direct blows. The contradictions of the [capitalist] world are concentrated in Asia, Africa and Latin America.[56]

Maoism thus not only denounced as 'imperialism' every form of economic or political influence of Western nations in third-world countries—itself a questionable proposition—but drew the conclusion that only a violent revolt of the peoples against their colonial masters could overthrow imperialist domination, which the Chinese saw as a conspiracy between foreign capital and the present ruling classes in the underdeveloped countries for the purpose of exploiting the broad masses. More recently the Soviet Union itself was ranked with the exploiting nations. In so far as orthodox Marxism–Leninism has become conservative and admitted the possibility of 'peaceful coexistence' between the two rival social systems, Chinese communism has departed further and further from its Russian prototype. The Chinese today see the USSR as no more than an accomplice of American capitalism and consequently as a new, still more dangerous variant of imperialism which will one day, like the others, have to be resisted by force of arms. Against this, China relies more and more on its own variant in the shape of a militant communism using dictatorial methods appropriate to a period of development, in competition and opposition to the orthodox Marxism-Leninism of the USSR and its satellites.

What the Maoist doctrine lacks in theoretical precision is made up for by its enthusiastic fighting spirit. Sober analysis is largely replaced by voluntaristic readiness for action at any cost. It may perhaps be wondered if this theory of imperialism is not primarily for internal consumption, as a means of integrating the vast masses of the Chinese people. But it cannot be overlooked that for many years the Chinese have consciously set out to court the third-world countries by means of large-scale propaganda designed to give practical reality to the theoretical postulate of an alliance with the ex-colonial peoples for the overthrow of capitalism. Nor can we dismiss as ineffectual Peking's continued criticism of official Marxism-Leninism, accusing the Soviet leaders of being the prey of an ossified bureaucratic mentality and mumbling old Marxist-Leninist formulae while in reality making common cause with the imperialists. Just because the Chinese ideology refrains from offering a universal theoretical basis, and instead calls on the masses with passionate enthusiasm to achieve particular goals, it has a special attraction for groups that are devoted to revolutionary action in the third world and also in the industrial countries. Chinese ideas in fact seem better suited to third-world conditions than do those of orthodox Marxism of either the Eastern or the Western variety. We need only refer to the life of Che Guevara, already interwoven with revolutionary legend, or, more specifically, to the skill with which Fidel Castro has succeeded in practicing a combination of the Russian and the Chinese strategies of anti-imperialism, relying heavily on the former's support, while effectively playing a game much closer to Chinese tactics.

It is also important that the Maoist variant of Lenin's theory of imperialism, with its emphasis on action and its belief that socialism will prevail first and foremost in the third world and not in the industrial countries with their strongly entrenched structures, has exerted considerable attraction on the 'New Left' and will no doubt continue to do so. There are innumerable examples of this. We may recall the mass demonstrations of American students in the early 1960s with the object of preventing recruitment of staff by the United Fruit Company, a vast concern which holds a key position in the agrarian economy of almost every Latin American country; not to mention the emotional partisanship of the New Left for the Vietminh during the Vietnam war, with its far-reaching indirect consequences. Again, the 'Red Army Fraction' operating in the Federal Republic of Germany justifies its terrorist actions on the ground that the armed struggle against the capitalist order in West Germany is part and parcel of the fight to liberate the third-world countries from imperialism. The Group's terrorist techniques and operations are directly modelled on the urban guerrilla strategy of the Tupamaros in South America.

It is hard to say how far the Maoist version of the theory of imperialism really regards war as a universal solution. Unlike the Soviet leaders, Mao apparently regarded the position of the imperialists, i.e., the capitalist West, as extremely weak. 'In substance, in the long run and from a strategic point of view, all imperialists and reactionaries must be regarded as paper tigers.' But one cannot fail to be concerned at the cold-bloodedness with which this and similar statements contemplate war—which in today's conditions must mean a world war—as a necessary means of liberation from imperialism.

Tilemann Grimm[57] has summed up the Maoist position as follows:

1. The revolutionary wars of all oppressed peoples are just and should be supported.
2. Despite the apparent strength of the imperialist forces, these wars are sure to be successful in the end.
3. The enemy is 'tactically dangerous' but 'strategically contemptible'.
4. An alliance with all revolutionary forces in the world is a *sine qua non* of the defeat of imperialism.
5. The atomic bomb and all imperialists and reactionaries are 'paper tigers'.
6. Final victory is, one may almost say, a matter of cosmic certainty.

The Maoist theory of imperialism is here completely transformed into a programme of political action, and, compared to the Marxist-Leninist position, has largely lost its value as an epistemological concept. While it must not be lost to view, it cannot serve as a tool for the critical understanding of historical facts. But it has had a powerful indirect effect on interpretations of imperialism in the third world, to which we shall return.

three

Provisional Assessment

It seems useful at this point to review the positions described so far and to draw up a kind of interim balance-sheet. In the foregoing chapters we have studied classical bourgeois theories of imperialism in the work of Hobson and Schumpeter and classical Marxist ones as expounded by Hilferding, Rosa Luxemburg and Lenin. We noted that later developments of the Marxist-Leninist position did not produce any basically new variants except for Maoism, which is unimpressive theoretically, however influential it may be in practice.

As regards Hobson and Schumpeter on the one hand and the Marxist writers on the other, we saw that their various theories were largely based on the experience of a particular period of industrial-capitalist development, which, as we know today, cannot be regarded as necessarily typical of capitalist systems in general. The years before 1914 were a time of extremely rapid economic growth, accompanied in the less developed countries by features of monopoly capitalism such as cartels, trusts, high protective tariffs and the economic domination of large banks. Comparable phenomena of course exist today, but in significantly varied forms. The extinction of the middle class, which these theories assumed by implication if not explicitly, has not come about in the expected form; the dominance of finance capital is even today far from complete, despite concentrations of capital on a far larger scale; and the capitalist system has retained its pluralist character to a much greater extent than would have been thought possible by either bourgeois or Marxist critics of imperialism before 1918. Capitalism has survived the world economic crisis of 1929–31 and the onslaught of fascism, nor does its existence seem to have been endangered by the liberation of former colonial territories, which is now almost complete, even if this liberation is more a political than an economic reality. The Marxist-Leninist prediction that the overthrow of imperialism must of necessity lead to the collapse, or as Lenin thought the irremediable decay, of capitalism has not yet proved correct or at any rate is not so manifest as had been expected.

Despite these evident facts, the Marxist-Leninist theory of imperialism still exerts considerable attraction by reason of its logical consistency. It is indeed gaining in popularity, either in the form of Maoism, which is not concerned with scientific rigour, or in the form of third-world anti-colonialism, with its emphasis on the widening gap between the industrial and the underdeveloped countries, or finally in the numerous forms of Western neo-Marxism, which we have still to examine. The Marxist-Leninist theory in its various forms is still of importance, moreover, to the study of non-communist Western views of imperialism, which cannot afford simply to ignore it, however dogmatic it may be judged to be. In the West we find a large number of positions which cannot be easily reduced to a common denominator, but all of which can be classified according to whether and how far they accept or reject Marxist-Leninist ideas as to the causes or nature of imperialism. While a number of neo-Marxist authors in the West have taken up the Leninist theory with the intent of further elaborating it, while, at the same time recognizing that the collapse of capitalism can no longer be taken for granted,[1] the great majority of non-communist writers implicitly or expressly take issue with both Hobson and Lenin. Some confine themselves to describing the latter's theories as one-sided, while others more or less accuse Hobson and Lenin of misrepresenting the facts, thereby painting a manifestly false picture of imperialism. One of these is David S. Landes, who in an article entitled 'Some Thoughts on the Nature of Economic Imperialism'[2] points out that economic factors are operating everywhere and not only in the case of social groups pursuing imperialist objectives. Any interpretation of imperialism from the economic point of view alone is unsatisfactory, according to Landes, because it 'will account for only a part—an important but nevertheless insufficient part—of the facts'. Economic motives existed in all camps, both those of the conquered and those of their rulers, but they do not by themselves provide an adequate explanation of imperialism. Similarly William L. Langer, an outstanding expert on the history of the imperialist age, has pointed out that 'Business interests may have an interest in the acquisition of territory, or they may not. But military and official classes almost always have.'[3] This quotation reflects a key feature of modern Western theories of imperialism, viz. the endeavour to bring economic factors within the framework of a more general interpretation in which political and social factors play a major part. Among theories of this kind various lines of thought can be distinguished, each of them emphasizing a different aspect.

four

More Recent Western Interpretations

1 Imperialism as extreme nationalism and as a phenomenon of power politics

Political variants of the classic theory of imperialism still enjoy much credit among Western researchers, though here again the emphasis has shifted. Prominence is given not to great-power interests dictated by *raison d'état* but to mass movements of nationalism in the industrial states, which were gradually being democratized; these movements were of course closely interwoven with antagonisms among the great powers, which they themselves helped to foment. It would certainly be wrong to underestimate popular nationalism as a motive force of modern imperialist domination, whether formal or informal. Today there is still a wide range of authors who maintain that imperialism was essentially a nationalist phenomenon. William L. Langer, as early as 1935, described British imperialism as basically 'a projection of nationalism beyond the boundaries of Europe'.[1] No empirical analysis of modern imperialism can ignore this factor. National enthusiasm and jingoism were certainly an important driving force; statesmen for their part were far less inclined to engage in costly overseas ventures than were those sections of the population, including the masses, who were tempted by vague prospects of future greatness and economic advantage for their own nation.

Had it not been for the nationalist enthusiasm for a forceful overseas policy, shared by the bourgeoisie and to some extent by the broad masses, the dominant élites would probably have been unable to persuade governments to pursue imperialist policies on the scale witnessed in the second half of the nineteenth and the early twentieth century, and which led to acute tension and conflicts among the powers themselves. The cost of administering dependent territories and of the steadily increasing armaments made necessary by growing rivalry among the powers was out of all proportion to the economic value of the newly acquired colonies. Statesmen were well aware of this, but a nationalist public opinion impelled them again and again to imperialist action, even at the risk of military complications.

Thus there are quite a number of writers who explain modern imperialism as essentially a product of the nationalist mass movements of the nineteenth century which, in the course of the development of Western societies, degenerated from liberalism to democratic totalitarianism. Hannah Arendt, in *The Origins of Totalitarianism*,[2] argued that the racist ideologies of imperialism and the anti-liberal structures of imperialist policy were a prelude to fascism, and she laid particular emphasis on the ideological affinity between imperialist and fascist ways of thought. Similarly George Lichtheim interprets imperialism as basically a product of extreme nationalism, manipulated to some extent by groups interested in imperial expansion for economic or other reasons:

> Imperialism as a movement—or, if one prefers, as an ideology—latched on to nationalism because no other popular base was available. But this statement can also be turned around: nationalism transformed itself into imperialism wherever the opportunity offered. It can be argued that popular patriotism was systematically corrupted when it passed into the service of the imperialist movement, but the speed with which the transformation was accomplished suggests that no deep resistance had to be overcome.[3]

David K. Fieldhouse took a similar view in his earlier works, especially his comparative account entitled *The Colonial Empires*.[4] Modern imperialism, he declared, was the product of a national mass hysteria which eventually took on the still more grotesque form of fascism. It was not businessmen and bankers but politicians who went with the stream and allowed their behaviour to be dictated by mass opinion. Capitalists were content to invest in economically sound projects regardless of whether these were located in the traditional industrial countries or in overseas territories, but politicians felt obliged to pander to the nationalist hysteria of the masses. The process of world-wide expansion, culminating in the 'scramble for Africa', was thus primarily a political phenomenon: the much-abused capitalists took no decisive part in the hectic competition for colonial territories.[5]

Unquestionably modern nationalism, as it developed with growing intensity in the European nation states from the 1870s onwards, was an important element in the ideology of imperialism.[6] But this in itself does not account for a great deal: for it was only in combination with economic factors, especially the enormously increased potential of the industrial states, that imperialism was able to deploy the tremendous expansive energies of its classic period after 1880.[7] It is true that nationalist urges of this kind often became independent of the conditions which had produced them and were thus a driving force of imperialism in their own right.[8] To this extent recent polemics against theories of imperialism based primarily on nationalist phenomena are superficial and not borne out by the evidence. It must be said, however, that as a rule it is impossible to ascribe any specific content to the nationalist programmes of expansion. The cry for a 'Greater Britain' or a 'Greater Germany' is seen on closer analysis to be an empty formula concealing a wide spectrum of imperialist motivations. Consequently an interpretation of imperialism as a form of exacerbated nationalism cannot in itself provide a satisfactory explanation of imperialism as a whole: it merely postpones a solution of the problem, as long as the roots of this nationalism itself have not been investigated.

The theory of imperialism as a form of intensified nationalism can provide a specific basis for enquiry in terms of the politico-social functions it has exercised in particular social contexts. In Britain, for instance, imperialist enthusiasm for a 'Greater Britain' played an important part as an element of social integration, by which the rising middle class was helped to find its place in a society still largely dominated by a conservative élite. This was even more the case in Imperial Germany, where the integral nationalism of the bourgeoisie was a reflection of their position between the conservative aristocracy on the one hand and the 'internationalist' working class on the other. From the point of view of the rising middle classes, however, imperialism was closely associated with the idea of modernization, legitimizing their claim to a proper share in the process of political decision-making, while at the same time fending off possible competition from the working class. Motivations such as these did much to strengthen the imperialist ideology, especially between 1880 and 1918.

Apart from this there has recently been a revival of interpretations of modern imperialism from the point of view of power politics, which in part derive expressly from Ranke's conception of history as the embodiment of the unending contest among great powers for self-assertion or hegemony. These interpretations are linked with the classic explanation of imperialist processes in terms of diplomatic history, such as the masterly work of William L. Langer.[9] They have also received some support from more recent works by R. Robinson and J. Gallagher, who interpret the official policy of Victorian imperialism chiefly in terms of power politics and strategy.[10] Robinson and Gallagher, it is true, regard political rivalries mainly as a factor tending to hasten imperialist processes; but motivations of the classic power-politics kind were in fact predominant in the 'official mind' of imperialism, as these authors show in the case of Great Britain. The interpretation of imperialism as a form of intensified rivalry within the international system can also derive some support from the systematizing efforts of political science. But the revival of such theories is dominated by the traditional approach in terms of diplomatic history, little attention being paid to aspects of home politics conducive to imperial expansion. This type of interpretation has of late been emphasized by Baumgart with reference to British and French imperialism, and it is not by chance that he refers expressly to statements about the nature of imperialism which date from the turn of the century.[11] In Baumgart's view imperialism is primarily a form of intensified great-power policy within the framework of a world-wide system, in which the maintenance and acquisition of power are seen as decisive factors of social change.[12] The advantage of this neo-Rankean conception lies in its applicability to power-political processes also at the present day; but its explanatory value is slight with regard to the highly complex processes of imperialism during its heyday.

It remains to be seen whether the new tendency will win general acceptance. For, while it must be admitted that the rivalries of the great powers stemming from their need to increase or maintain their power may in some cases play, or have played, a self-generating role, they do not suffice to account for the extraordinary dynamic force of imperialism. Theories of this kind in fact make absolute what is no more than one factor among others: it certainly has an accelerating effect on imperialist processes, induced either by internal or by peripheral causes, but it does not itself originate them. In general the urge for increased power cannot be regarded as a specific cause of imperialist processes. The weakness of this theoretical approach is shown clearly by the fact that power-political and strategic motives generally do not come prominently into play until the manifold forms of indirect or informal imperialist penetration have proved to be unavailing. All recent research goes to show that statesmen and diplomats have nearly always been 'reluctant imperialists', impelled by circumstances rather than by any positive aims of their own. This makes it reasonable to conclude that the neo-Rankean theory of imperialism has little explanatory force, at least as far as the causation of imperialist processes is concerned.

2 *Objectivist theories*

A second group of interpretations tends to represent imperialism as an objective process due fundamentally to the unavoidable impact of advanced Western civilization on the comparatively backward native cultures of the third world: imperialism is thus the inevitable concluding phase of the long-term process of the spread of Western civilization all over the globe. Herbert Lüthy has expressed this point of view forcefully, in opposition to the one-sided condemnation of imperialism by economic theoreticians in particular; he interprets the process of colonization and its final imperialist phase as a necessary stage in the evolution of a world-wide civilization based on modern technology.[13] Colonization was 'not a philanthropic educational institution', but it was nevertheless a work of education, in many areas at least, leading to the Europeanization of the peoples of the third world. Lüthy points out that the ex-colonial peoples themselves show no desire to undo the basic effects of this secular process, and that it is therefore out of place to maintain an attitude of moral self-criticism in respect of the colonial past.

British colonial policy in the age of Lord Lugard in fact endeavoured to preserve as far as possible the social structures and cultures of the indigenous peoples, but in the long run this policy proved both unsuccessful and retrograde; by contrast, in the light of hindsight, the French policy of ruthless assimilation seems to have been the right one. Lüthy sees colonization as essentially the triumph of Western civilization over the ancient social orders of Africa and Asia—a process carried forward by thousands of colonists, pioneers and adventurers representing, as it were, the surplus energies of the West. 'This outburst of surplus energy was the true motive force against which the antiquated, crumbling or petrified political and social systems of the non-European world were shattered or fell to pieces.'[14] The economic interests of the Western industrial states had as little to do with this as had aggressive nationalism. This is proved by the 'grotesque disproportion between the material forces deployed by the Western powers and the effects they produced': the third-world societies succumbed with scarcely a struggle to the onslaught of a handful of European invaders and adventurers.

Scarcely anywhere did the colonists encounter political and social structures that possessed any inner power of resistance; scarcely anywhere did they confront peoples who felt they had any freedom or independence worth defending or who cared for the difference between one ruler and another.

That which today stands up against colonial domination is itself the work of colonizers.[15]

The extraordinary weakness of the pre-colonial cultures is thus an imperative reason for not interpreting colonization and imperialism exclusively in terms of the overriding economic or political interests of the European powers. These generally came on the scene only when the power vacuum in overseas territories left them no choice but to intervene in order to put a stop to 'general plunder and piracy', and by degrees to impose order on chaotic conditions. Colonization was thus far from being merely the exploitation of conquered peoples: it was primarily a work of education and civilization. 'Wherever colonial policy sought an inner justification over and above the mere exercise of power, it regarded its mission as an educative work aimed at final emancipation.'[16] Lüthy rejects no less emphatically the idea that imperialism brutally destroyed rich native cultures. When the European world order collapsed it was for European reasons and not because of any resistance by the colonial peoples. 'For the non-European world in general the period of the colonial empires was one of peace and security such as the Asians and Africans had scarcely ever known throughout their bloodstained history.'[17]

These arguments amount to an unmistakable apologia for Western policy. Lüthy wastes no time on the contention of some modern researchers that imperialism itself to a large extent created the state of underdevelopment out of which the third-world countries have painfully extricated themselves or in which they are still imprisoned. His analysis of colonialism is, instead, accompanied by a severe criticism of Europeans for having themselves destroyed, in two world wars, the 'material, political and moral foundations of Europe's predominance in the world'.[18] As regards third-world liberation movements, Lüthy remarks tersely that they constitute 'a revolt not by people who want to be different, but by those who feel themselves to be like their masters or impatiently wish to become so'.[19] But the moral slant of this criticism is wrong. The 'revolt' was not something superfluous, the mere acceleration of a process that was already taking place: it was a necessity if the third-world peoples were effectively to throw off the tutelage of European rulers and create their own culture. However, Lüthy is justified in his basic viewpoint that the objective historical consequences of the colonialist era and its final imperialist phase should be appraised without sentimentality and that in some respects they were beneficial to the indigenous peoples also.[20]

A similar attempt has been made by David Landes to assess the nature of imperialism as an objective phenomenon that was bound to come about in any case, so that the explanation 'transcends place and circumstance'.[21] Landes vigorously attacks the economic interpretation of imperialism in its many variants. These, he says, may indeed throw light on important causal connections, but they break down when confronted with actual facts. 'Businessmen at home . . . entertained far less illusions about the profitability of colonial ventures than the adventurers, chauvinists and statesmen who exhorted them to invest and become rich.'[22] Economic factors were certainly at work everywhere, but they applied to the colonized peoples as well as the colonizers. The initiative in imperialist expansion was generally taken by marginal groups of the community—colonists, adventurers and politicians—who succeeded in mobilizing in their favour the authorities and resources of their own state, or sometimes of a foreign power, frequently by simply appealing to national prestige. Imperialism in fact arose wherever an imbalance of power—be it political, military, cultural or economic—invited the stronger party for the time being to exercise domination over the weaker. 'It seems to me that one has to look at imperialism as a multifarious response to a common opportunity that consists simply in disparity of power. Whenever and wherever such disparity has existed, people and groups have been ready to take advantage of it.'[23] The relation between powers of unequal strength is always unstable. The weaker party is never prepared to acknowledge his inferiority, because of the material disadvantages and above all the moral humiliation which this entails. The stronger, on the other hand, must always take heed for his own security, and this generally means enlarging his empire.

This type of explanation in many ways resembles the political theory of imperialism as it was developed by the neo-Rankeans around the turn of the century; but it is much more broadly based and comprises important new aspects. When Landes speaks of the imbalance of power, he does not only mean state power in the traditional sense but the sum of political, economic, technological and cultural resources which constitute the historical driving-force of large social entities. This definition also includes indirect forms of domination, whether cultural, economic or technological, or any other bonds of 'influence' such as exist in the world today and determine relationships between the industrial and the underdeveloped countries. The effect of Landes's argument is contrary to the tendency in Western countries to feel that they have, so to speak, regained a state of innocence as far as imperialism is concerned, despite the continued existence of imperialist dependence in many forms as between the industrial and underdeveloped regions of the earth. On the other hand, Landes's definition is too abstract and general to be an adequate expression of actual processes. In the last resort the 'imbalance of power' is one of the tautological formulae by which the interpretation of modern imperialism is beset whenever it attempts to define its theme in universal terms.

3 Socio-economic theories

The great majority of Western theories of imperialism tend to see it not as a necessary phase of the capitalist system as such but rather as the result of particular social structures and combinations of interests arising from the impact of modern capitalism on pre-industrial societies. Most of these interpretations derive in one form or another from Schumpeter's classic treatise, and partly also from Max Weber's distinction between normal free-market capitalism and the 'predatory', monopolistic kind based on exploiting overseas territories. The true sources of imperialism are thus not so much the economic interests of finance capital and export-oriented industry, as the politico-social interests of groups which saw their social status threatened by the advance of democracy—although these groups were frequently allied with sections of heavy industry and others especially interested in imperialist exploitation.

Schumpeter's thesis that imperialism was a specific product of outdated, anachronistic forms of domination and social structures, and thus represented an 'atavistic' trend in modern, egalitarian, industrial societies, is supported by the school of thought we are now discussing with new arguments of a more purely sociological as opposed to a socio-psychological kind. The argument that—contrary to Lenin's assumption—capitalist industrial society of the liberal type is essentially cosmopolitan and based on international exchange is not revived simply because it serves to absolve the capitalist system and pluralist industrial society of the Western type from all sins of the past. On the contrary, those who argue thus are convinced that Western constitutional democracy is in principle able to divest itself of all imperialist leanings, and that capitalism has no intrinsic need of imperial outlets and investment opportunities. Keynes, developing Hobson's arguments, pointed out that a democratic state could direct the economy of a Western industrial society in such a way as to enable it completely to reject imperialism.

Arguments such as these are by no means used only by those who feel the need to defend an actual state of affairs, but also by thinkers who fervently desire to bring about a thorough democratization of political and social conditions in a spirit of liberal humanism. One of these is Hannah Arendt, who denounced all forms of modern totalitarianism and traced its roots to the imperialist practices and ideologies of the late nineteenth century. Like Schumpeter, though starting from different premisses, Hannah Arendt concluded that imperialism is caused in the last resort by residual elements of pre-democratic social structures which have survived in modern industrial societies.

In a somewhat cruder and naïver way, E. M. Winslow has also described imperialism as due to relics of feudal and militaristic attitudes in Western industrial society.[24] His interpretation tends ultimately to justify neo-liberal economic policies and the informal and unobtrusive domination of the world by the great industrial nations. Winslow believes that the abolition of traditional hierarchical structures would remove the specific stimuli which brought about imperialism as a system of forcible expansion and foreign domination; this view is shared by thinkers who are otherwise less inclined than he to absolve capitalism as such, not to speak of the higher bourgeoisie, of all responsibility for the imperialist excesses of the past. Not all of them argue so superficially as Walther Sulzbach,[25] another follower of Schumpeter who goes even further than Winslow in exculpating the democratic present at the expense of the nationalist and imperialist past. Sulzbach takes the view that imperialism is a specific product of modern nationalism, which in turn owes its origin to the combative attitudes which predominated in monarchical European states but now belong to the past. It would suffice, in his opinion, to do away with ideological survivals of bygone social structures to put an end to imperialism with its aggressive, resentful and warlike instincts.

Most Western students of the problem, however, do

not suggest such an easy way out as do Winslow and Sulzbach. Walt Whitman Rostow, for instance, adopts quite a different position in his well-known work *The Stages of Economic Growth*, [26] which is intended to offer an alternative to the Marxist theory of historical development as it relates to modern industrial society. Rostow does not dispute that at certain stages economic factors have done much to bring about imperialist expansion and imperialist wars. Both in their initial and in their maturer phases, industrial societies have often been tempted by economic opportunities overseas. But—and here Rostow joins issue with the Marxist position—imperialist expansion is in principle of only marginal importance to the development of modern industrial societies, which do not really need imperialism at all. On the other hand Rostow concedes that gross disparities in economic growth, combined with wide differences in military potential, tend to favour aggressive policies of a regional or global nature. However, imperialist expansion is in his view by no means peculiar to industrial capitalism, but is generally due to non-economic and especially political factors. Here Rostow, like Schumpeter, assigns a major role to traditionalist factors such as the political roles of groups whose elevated social status dates from pre-industrial times. A mature capitalist consumer society, on the other hand, shows no tendency towards imperialism, and in principle capitalism, despite Lenin's view, has no need of imperialism in order to survive. On the contrary, 'while colonialism is virtually dead, capitalism in the Western hemisphere, Western Europe and Japan is enjoying an extraordinary surge of growth'.[27]

This theory does not touch on the question how far informal types of economic predominance, not associated with direct political control, should be classified as imperialist. Rostow's view of imperialism is a restrictive one, clearly designed to defend capitalism of the modern type against the charge that it must in all circumstances lead to imperialism. On the other hand Rostow can justly contend that his Marxist opponents have always underrated the elasticity of capitalism as an economic system and have failed to recognize its capacity to expand phenomenally without the need to exploit more or less undeveloped overseas territories.

Western theorists do not deny that the economic possibilities which imperialism afforded to the European industrial countries have been of considerable importance to the growth of capitalism itself. But recent researchers for the most part do not share the Marxist view that imperialism was a *conditio sine qua non* for the development of capitalism—a view put forward in cautious but stimulating terms in a recent work by Eric Hobsbawm.[28] Albert Imlah, in *Economic Elements in the 'Pax Britannica',*[29] concedes that the abundant overseas resources of the British economy helped it to survive periods of crisis, and that imperialist expansion in general speeded up economic growth. S. B. Saul has also pointed out that the extensive system of international trade which Britain, as the leading Western industrial power, created within and outside the Empire did much to promote the emergence of a multilateral economic system and thus of world trade.[30] But both these authors are far from postulating a necessary link between capitalist growth and the development of overseas economic opportunities by means of imperialist policies. All the views discussed in this section have in common that they seek to integrate the economic factors involved in imperialism into the more general framework of a theory of social development which emphasizes the part played by the activist groups that had actually been behind colonialist and imperialist policies, instead of indulging in grandiose theories whose truth or otherwise is scarcely capable of empirical verification.

4 The theory of free-trade imperialism

The most significant innovation in the development of Western theories of imperialism is no doubt the concept of 'informal imperialism'. By recognizing that there are numerous informal types of imperialist domination which precede or accompany the establishment of formal rule, or even make it unnecessary, Western thinking on the subject of imperialism has drawn closer to Marxist theory: the latter has always been based on the premiss that imperialism is primarily a function of the capitalist system at a particular stage of its development, and is therefore not essentially a nationalist phenomenon, although it makes use of the power of national states to secure its ends.[31] Generally speaking, most non-Marxist theoreticians admit nowadays that dependency of an imperialist sort may well result from the most varied kinds of informal influence, especially of an economic nature. Imperialist forces at the colonial periphery were by no means obliged constantly to resort to the actual use of political power: it was generally quite enough to know that the imperialist groups could count on support from the metropolitan power in the event of a crisis. Formal political rule thus appears only as the most specific, but not the normal type of imperialist dependence.

The pioneer study on these lines is 'The Imperialism of Free Trade'[32] by Ronald Robinson and John Gallagher, which has become a classic. The authors of this essay began by opposing their theory of 'free-trade imperialism' to the traditional chronology of British imperialism. The older view was that after a period of disintegration of the old colonial empires under the influence of Manchester liberalism, whose anti-imperialism found expression in the grant of self-government to considerable parts of the former empire, there ensued in the early 1880s a qualitatively new period of neo-imperialism. Robinson and Gallagher took issue with this view, stressing instead the continuity of British imperial policy from the beginning of the nineteenth century. The territorial growth of the British Empire itself bore witness to a steady process of imperialist expansion, pursued constantly although with varying methods which included those of both 'formal' and 'informal' rule. True, Victorian imperialism generally confined itself to using the power of the British state to safeguard its own trade, although no longer with mercantilist objectives as had been the case before 1810; but the Victorians never hesitated to employ forms of political domination when economic interests were seriously threatened. As Robinson and Gallagher put it: 'British policy followed the principle of extending control informally if possible and formally if necessary. To label the one method "anti-imperialist" and the other "imperialist" is to ignore the fact that whatever the method British interests were steadily safeguarded and extended.'[33]

By developing the theory of 'informal empire' Robinson and Gallagher broke decisively with the tradition which defined imperialism exclusively in terms of formal territorial colonial rule, and instead emphasized the importance of imperialist factors of a non-governmental character. The true motive force of Victorian expansion was economic, and the imperialists were at first content to exercise informal control from a few coastal stations. Political methods were in the main used only to open up previously closed markets to the ostensibly free operation of Western competitive capitalism. Preference was as a rule given to informal methods of economic expansion, but from early Victorian times Britain resorted to formal imperialist rule whenever this seemed necessary in order to protect economic interests which would otherwise appear to be threatened. 'The usual summing up of the policy of the free trade empire as "trade, not rule" should read "trade with informal control if possible; trade with rule when necessary".'[34]

The chief significance of this theory is that it regards methods of economic expansion which, formally speaking, are in accordance with the rules of the marketplace as no less imperialistic than other forms of indirect influence, including the use of all kinds of indirect methods to establish hegemony or indirect control. Such methods have in common the fact that they generally do not require direct recourse to political power, which indeed is only appealed to in the last resort. British overseas expansion appears as a continuous process of the extension of, primarily, economic influence, with only the occa-

sional use of political force. The switch to formal colonial rule in the later phase from 1880 onwards is attributed primarily to increasing rivalries among the
European great powers, which prevented the continuance of older types of 'informal' imperialist rule with a
minimum display of metropolitan power.

The theory of 'informal empire' raises considerable
problems, both theoretical and practical, and has not
been accepted without dispute by other scholars, but it
has had a profound effect on the development of modern
Western theories of imperialism: for it appeared to offer
the possibility of finding a common explanation for a
variety of elements which had hitherto been regarded as
isolated factors. These are, in particular: the process of
almost unnoticed overseas expansion, promoted by individual ambitious adventurers, businessmen and specula-
tors; the dynamic expansion of a rapidly developing capitalist system; and the high-imperialist phase of formal
territorial expansion supported, from the early 1880s, by
the nationalist fervour of large sections of the home population. The theory was thus well suited to explain both
the continuous acquisition of overseas territories since
the eighteenth century, which was due to forces operating at the periphery, and the feverish expansionism of
the last two decades before 1914.

The striking feature of the new conception was that
economic expansion on a free-trade basis and political
expansion by means either of informal hegemony or of
formal colonial rule were seen as two aspects of one and
the same process. In mid-Victorian times, Robinson and
Gallagher observe, 'the combination of commercial penetration and political influence allowed the United King-

dom to command those economies which could be made to fit best into her own'.[35] In general it was not so much a consciously planned operation as a spontaneous process resulting from the exuberance of Britain's economic strength. It was noteworthy that statesmen for their part nearly always preferred, when possible, to avoid any further extension of direct colonial rule.

Robinson and Gallagher distinguish between the 'informal empire', as the area in which British trade and overseas investments achieved a dominant economic position, and, on the other hand, colonial territories and dominions subject to formal imperialist rule in the narrower sense, supported by the apparatus of political power. On this definition, the 'informal empire' comprised in the first instance all areas that could, directly or indirectly, be called colonial territories, but also regions which might in modern parlance be regarded as already developed. These include formally sovereign nations in so far as they clearly belonged to the sphere of influence of an imperial power: for instance, the South American states, which, the authors point out, became a highly important field of activity for British informal imperialism after 1810, being a preferred area for large-scale foreign investment. Among the primary instruments of informal imperialism, Robinson and Gallagher cite the institution of intensive trade relations, in which the technological advantages of the home country were brought to bear; the penetration of the peripheral economy by means of large-scale overseas investment; and the process by which indigenous ruling circles and interest groups were persuaded to co-operate with the metropolis. Even in such areas it was by no means unknown for formal power to be used also, especially when it was a question of opening up overseas territories to British commerce or, in the free-trade era, to Western trade in general.

The theory of free-trade imperialism as formulated by Robinson and Gallagher has been attacked on various grounds. It was pointed out, firstly, that the classic doctrine of free trade could not be simply identified with informal imperialism, if only because its protagonists, such as Cobden, were opposed to imperialism in any form.[36] Other critics disputed the contention that, whenever informal methods of imperialist expansion proved insufficient, British policy always resorted to political pressure, political influence or territorial control. D. C. M. Platt,[37] in particular, pointed out that British traders or investors in critical situations were not generally able to rely on political help from their motherland. He showed in detail that, on the contrary, British governments generally showed great reluctance when urged to use political means to further or protect the economic interests of British merchants, bankers or bond-holders in overseas countries. This, according to Platt, was especially true of Latin America, and it was therefore absurd to speak of Britain exercising 'informal control' over Argentina from the 1820s onward.

Platt and other writers also challenged the 'continuity theory' advanced by Robinson and Gallagher. In the 1880s, they argued, imperialist expansion took on a different character in the sense that territories were acquired as an insurance against the future, even though no immediate economic interests were involved. Geoffrey Barraclough remarks that imperialist expansion, especially when considered from a general European standpoint, took on a quite new and much more aggressive character. Up to the 1880s the initiative for territorial expansion had generally come from interested business groups at home and at the periphery; governments as a rule preferred to let commercial companies go ahead, granting them a royal charter and hence protection in case of need, but otherwise keeping rather in the background. Now, however, the position was gradually reversed, as governments were pressed to annex overseas territories even though the immediate commercial involvement of their own nationals in the areas concerned was negligible. Business sectors which expected to profit from monopolistic concessions began to crusade for annexation at any price; the slogan 'Trade follows the flag' became increasingly popular, though not a few left-wing writers disputed its validity. Governments were urged to acquire overseas territories on the ground that, however unviable they might be economically for the time being, they could sooner or later be turned into remunerative colonies: it was important for the nation to secure them, even at a heavy loss, so as to benefit from their alleged economic potential. Rosebery's phrase 'pegging out claims for posterity' reflected a strong consensus within the middle and upper classes in support of pre-emptive territorial acquisitions.

The concept of 'informal imperialism' thus needs to be defined with greater precision than hitherto, and we shall do well to treat it with some caution. The basic problem of its use is that it does not answer the question where to draw a line between imperialism properly so called and market relationships between countries of different economic potential. So far investigation of this point has not yielded precise results. David Landes has remarked by way of warning that not every form of dependency leading to the exploitation of native populations or the working class is to be equated with imperialism: such a wholesale definition would make serious research impossible. Instead he proposes to define imperialism in a way which explicitly links it with formal or informal political control: 'Imperialist exploitation consists in the employment of labour at wages lower than would obtain in a free bargaining situation; or in the appropriation of goods at prices lower than would obtain in a free market. Imperialist exploitation, in other words, implies non-market constraint.'[38] Recent studies, however, have not as yet followed this line, but have contented themselves with a more or less summary use of the notion of 'informal imperialism' or 'free-trade imperialism'.

5 Socio-imperialist theories

The theory of 'informal imperialism', superseding the old definition of imperialism as the imposition of colonial rule in the narrower sense, has made a breach in former arguments and opened the way to new developments in the theory of imperialism. In American studies the theory of informal or free-trade imperialism has been taken up especially by William Appleman Williams and Walter LaFeber. These authors treat American imperialism as a continuous process beginning with the settlement of the North American continent and continuing with U.S. efforts to secure and maintain an 'open door' in countries beyond the Atlantic and the Pacific. The brief interlude of overt imperialism between 1898 and 1900 is treated as a temporary deviation from the main path of development, due to various factors including especially the recession of 1896 and consequent fears of an economic crisis. Since then the United States, despite its anti-imperialist ideology, has consistently pursued a policy of free-trade imperialism with the object of opening up the whole world to the products and capital of the technologically superior U.S. economy.[39]

Hans-Ulrich Wehler has made use of these studies and certain patterns of behaviour deduced from the American experience, particularly Williams's formula of the 'consensus' of all socially important groups and ruling circles that the U.S. economy and society needed continuous economic expansion to preserve its stability and avert revolution. On this basis, and in the context of Bismarck's colonial policy, Wehler developed a new theory analogous to the 'informal empire' described by Robinson and Gallagher but combined with the conception of 'unequal economic growth', and thus drawing heavily upon the findings of modern economic theory.[40] Wehler agrees that only a gradual and not a substantive difference can be perceived between the methods of overseas expansion in the free-trade era and those of direct imperialism in and after the 1880s; but he interprets modern imperialism as essentially the result of the interruptions and fluctuations of economic growth in the European industrial countries during the 'great depression', i.e., the period from 1873 onwards. The experience of periodic crises gave birth to an 'ideological consensus' that the economy must be furnished with new overseas markets at any cost, so that it could continue to produce goods and expand in times of economic crisis, as otherwise the whole social fabric might be endangered.

The concept of imperialism underlying this interpretation is both wider and narrower than traditional theories. It is narrower in so far as it seeks the causes of imperialist policy chiefly in the economic field. According to Wehler, imperialism is the result of a fundamental disequilibrium in world economic development since the industrial revolution, and of the violent fluctuations of economic growth in the industrial states. In Wehler's terminology 'imperialism' covers any form of expansion, even when this takes place exclusively according to the formal rules of the free marketplace. A policy of systematically promoting exports, for instance, seems to him a typical form of imperialism, at all events when it is directed primarily at markets in underdeveloped countries. To this extent Wehler's use of the term is wider than that traditionally used. He defines imperialism as 'that species of direct-formal or indirect-informal control which the Western industrial states, under the pressure of industrialization resulting in specific economic, social and political problems, have, thanks to their superiority in many fields, extended over less developed regions of the globe'.[41] This definition, however, is so broad and elastic that it would probably be difficult, with its aid alone, to derive any profound insight from the historical material. On closer analysis it appears to embrace a plurality of concepts of imperialism which are not really combined into a consistent explanatory pattern. Many points remain obscure or undecided: for instance the question whether economic or technological superiority is bound to result in imperialism, or whether and how far political influence must come into play so as to transform relationships of dependency based on the rules of the marketplace into relationships of an imperialist character.

More decisive is the fact that Wehler expresses himself ambiguously as to the objective significance of economic factors. At times he appears to regard imperialist expansion—whether merely the informal promotion of exports or the establishment of more or less direct colonial rule—as performing the function of a kind of business-cycle policy, but he hesitates to draw the logical conclusion from this view. For it is undisputed that the establishment of overseas colonies was of no significance in the short term (if indeed it was at any time) from the point of view of reviving business at home in times of economic recession. In most cases, certainly in Germany, imperialism was never a paying proposition economically for the community as a whole, though it was often (but by no means always) extremely profitable to the groups directly involved. It is not by accident, therefore, that, while Wehler's theory sets out to give priority to economic factors, it shifts imperceptibly into a partly sociological, partly socio-psychological vein. On close examination the chief motive force of imperialist policy proves to consist not in the objective economic advantages of informal or formal imperialist control, but only in the subjective expectation of such advantages in the future. Wehler himself does not deny that the opening up of colonial territories was of only marginal importance for the economic growth of modern industrial societies, and that purely economic explanations of imperialism are erroneous if argued on the basis of the economic data. He therefore has recourse to an auxiliary theory already put forward by William A. Williams, viz., that as a consequence of uneven economic growth there emerged among the dominant classes of German society an 'ideological consensus' as to the need for an expansionist policy in order to ensure continuous economic growth. This ignores to an unnecessary extent the fact that there had been at the time enormous differences of opinion concerning the methods and objectives of imperialist policy. According to Wehler, however, the dominant classes were at one in calling for economic expansion by whatever means, because it was generally supposed that otherwise the social fabric might be undermined and revolution might break out. To this extent imperialism was not only a policy designed to smooth out variations in the trade cycle and provide for continuous economic growth, but also a strategy whereby the ruling élite sought to defend the social order against elements rising from below and to maintain their own privileged position. From this point of view Wehler defines modern imperialism, regardless of accessory economic factors, as 'social imperialism', i.e., a policy by which established élites seek to defend their privileges in a society exposed to substantial change as a consequence of industrialization: the objective threat is here mixed with subjective fears in such a way that they are hard to disentangle.

Wehler sought detailed confirmation of this theory in the history of Bismarck's colonial policy. Bismarck's chief motive in advocating a formal colonial policy was, he argues, to split the liberal opposition and thus keep it from power. In short, his imperialism was dictated by domestic politics: the policy of colonial acquisitions was in the last resort a form of 'manipulated social imperialism' with the object of defending the conservative social structure and, not least, his own 'Bonapartist dictatorship' against the rising tide of modernization, while suppressing or thwarting all political movements that in any way opposed his purpose.

It is interesting that Wehler has to resort to auxiliary constructions of a socio-psychological kind in order to link together the economic and the socio-conservative elements of his theory of imperialism. For the concept of an 'ideological consensus' proves on closer inspection to be a socio-psychological one, serving to bridge the manifest gap in Wehler's theory between objective economic circumstances on the one hand and politico-sociological motives of imperialist expansionism on the other. The socio-psychological disposition of ruling classes in favour of such expansion—whether based on the belief that it is the only way to ensure continuous economic growth, or whether as a means of defending their endangered social position—frequently asserts itself independently of objective economic factors, and it is from this standpoint that Wehler views the question. To this extent his theory of 'social imperialism', which was initially based on economic considerations first and foremost, is transformed somewhat unexpectedly into a socio-psychological pattern, the prime motive of imperialism being seen in the disposition of dominant classes to promote imperial expansion in order to bolster their own privileged position at home. In this way, although 'social imperialism' originated in the time of the 'great depression' after 1873, Wehler is able to apply it to later periods and in particular to Germany after 1896, although by that time the economic climate had fundamentally changed and there was little question of any interruption of economic growth, at any rate not of the same magnitude. Wehler's theory appears ultimately to be an eclectic one: it combines several disparate forms of explanation in a manner not free from ambiguity, so that one or another can be brought into the foreground according to the context of the argument. The core of the theory, however, is that imperialism is a strategy practised by the ruling élites of traditionalist societies in order to protect their privileged position, threatened by the development of industrial society and especially the rise of democratic and socialist movements.

Wehler's theory of 'social imperialism' may justly be regarded as the most radical example of an 'endogenous' theory, i.e., one which looks for the causes of imperialist expansion solely within Western industrial societies themselves. However, it does not, like the Marxists, discern these causes primarily in objective economic facts, but in the interplay of economic, social and political factors. 'Social imperialism', in Wehler's view, is as it were a result of the secular process of modernization, which dissolves the social and economic structure of traditional societies and prompts the dominant classes to seek diversionary strategies, an endeavour in which they are closely allied with the ascendant interests of capitalism.

6 Peripheral theories of imperialism

In opposition to all theories which regard imperialism as the product of economic, social or socio-psychological processes within the industrial states themselves, there has recently appeared a contingent of critics who, on the contrary, see it as originating in the main from developments in the overseas territories which came under European rule. According to these critics, it was crises on the periphery and not in Europe which provided the main impetus for, at least, the period of formal imperialism after 1880. This view was expressed in the early 1960s by Robinson and Gallagher, who, with some modification of their earlier standpoint, observed that: 'Scanning Europe for the causes, the theorists of imperialism have been looking for the answers in the wrong places. The crucial changes that set all working took place in Africa itself.'[42]

The theses of Hobson or the various schools of Marxism, as well as such Western theorists as Leonard Woolf or Hans-Ulrich Wehler, are described by these critics as 'one-eyed analyses'[43]—one-sidedly Eurocentric theories which ignore important aspects and particularly the part played by indigenous peoples and their political élites. The older theories, according to Robinson, were based on a gross illusion in so far as they assumed that all active components of the imperialist process were necessarily European, while leaving out of account equally vital non-European factors.[44] At the same time these critics have, to some extent, revived the older political theory of imperialism, while altering its emphasis. As a rule, they maintain, it was not a matter of consciously aiming to build new empires or enlarge existing ones; what took place was rather a cumulative process of preventive annexations and, in the case of the *beati possidentes*, measures intended to protect and stabilize the colonial possessions they already had. In their book *Africa and the Victorians*,[45] Robinson and Gallagher laid important foundations for this new interpretation. Their analysis of the critical phase of European imperialism, the 'scramble for Africa' in the last four decades before 1914, challenged the traditional theory of the motives behind this process. In what they called 'the official mind of imperialism', they found few signs of the motivations which had hitherto generally been ascribed to statesmen of the period. Although the latter gave the public to understand that the acquisition of colonial territories was useful to the domestic economy or necessary for the defence of existing colonies, history showed that with few exceptions they took a hesitant and mistrustful view of imperialist expansion. In the case of Britain their dominant motive was the strategic protection of the existing empire and above all the route to India. To this extent the growing rivalry among the European powers was a decisive stimulant to further expansion and particularly the transformation of informal into formal rule. It was extremely rare, however, for anything like a 'grand design' to come into play. The imperialist actions of the great powers were generally provoked by crises in third-world territories, which were shaken to their foundations by the effects of informal imperialist penetration with the collaboration of native élites, thus creating a danger of intervention by rival European powers.

It might naturally be asked why late-Victorian states-men pursued a policy of expansion in many areas, including some which promised little economic advantage, although they were in principle no less mistrustful of imperial expansion than their predecessors. The question, however, is to some extent wrongly directed. 'The answer is to be found first in the nationalist crises in Africa itself, which were the work of intensifying European influences during previous decades; and only secondly in the interlocking of these crises in Africa with rivalries in Europe.'[46] Along with 'peripheral' factors (a term introduced by Fieldhouse), the decisive causes were political, economic ones being only subsidiary. Robinson and Gallagher also remark that 'any theory of imperialism grounded on the notion of a single decisive cause is too simple for the complicated historical reality of the African partition'.[47] From the 1880s onwards economic expansion tended to follow territorial expansion: economic arguments were generally adduced as afterthoughts to justify territorial gains that had already taken place. 'The arguments of the so-called new imperialism were *ex post facto* justifications of advances, they were not the original reasons for making them.'[48]

This position has recently been developed and systematically argued in David K. Fieldhouse's *Economics and Empire 1830–1914.*[49] In this work the traditional 'Eurocentric' theories are formally opposed by a theory of 'peripheral imperialism', which concentrates on developments in the colonies themselves. The traditional theories are subjected to damaging criticism in the light of actual events in Asia and Africa during the colonial period. Statistical evidence is adduced to refute economic theories as to the necessity of overseas markets for the purpose of expanding national trade or world trade, and likewise those which postulate overseas investment as essential to the survival of capitalism. Starting from the premiss, admittedly open to question, that imperialist policies only benefited national trade if accompanied by protectionist measures, Fieldhouse shows that in almost all cases the metropolitan powers traded with their own colonies to a relatively insignificant extent, and that this trade actually tended to diminish during the heyday of imperialism. As to the need for overseas investment opportunities, Fieldhouse argues, as others have done, that there was no direct correlation between such investment and territorial expansion. Without disputing that economic factors were at work, he denies that they suffice to account for the vast process of expansion of the European industrial states all over the globe; much less was colonial expansion necessary for the historical development of capitalism itself.

Fieldhouse, who in his earlier works followed the political theory of imperialism, still accepts it in its various forms but has modified it in the light of this new approach. Considerations of prestige played an important part, but in general statesmen had no grandiose plans of imperial expansion: it was usually a question of accumulating preventive measures designed to safeguard real or supposed national interests against encroachment by rival nations. 'Thus imperialism was generated by the caution, rather than the belligerence, of the "official mind" in its attempt to protect national interests in a period of unavoidable change.' It was often the case, especially with French imperialism, that 'colonies provided a safety-valve not . . . for surplus manufactures, but for the enterprise and bellicosity of the jingoists and traditional fighting castes'.[50]

Decisive importance attached, on the other hand, to events in third-world territories which undermined or destroyed the older forms of informal European influence and made necessary the establishment of formal colonial rule. Imperialism was not primarily the result of developments in the industrial countries but was rather a 'reaction to unsatisfactory conditions on the periphery'.[51] The establishment of formal rule must be regarded as a 'response by the metropolitan powers to external stimuli',[52] and it is vain to seek its causes in economic or other processes in the metropolis itself.

The principle thus expressed in uncompromising terms is qualified to some extent in Fieldhouse's further argument, which contains observations that are certainly of great value to the subject. He distinguishes two main forms of 'peripheral imperialism', which differ widely in character. On the one hand is the 'sub-imperialism' of 'men on the spot'; on the other, formal imperialism, which comes about as the inevitable result of the collapse of traditional methods of more or less informal co-operation between native élites and the Europeans concerned, in the manner typical of the era of free-trade colonialism.

As regards 'sub-imperialism', it is hard to overestimate the importance of the part it has played in the historic process of the spread of Western civilization over the globe. Especially in the case of France, but also in many British territories, it was the white settlers, merchants, soldiers and diplomats who relentlessly pushed forward the process of territorial acquisition, usually on their own initiative and often against the express wishes of their home governments. An outstanding instance is the part played by Cecil Rhodes and the British South Africa Company. Fieldhouse here refers to the older concept of the 'turbulent frontier' as put forward by John Kenneth Galbraith.[53] Local conflicts with indigenous populations on the periphery—whether provoked by the white settlers, or because the natives took up arms of their own accord—constantly gave rise to an extension of territorial control by the imperialists on the ground of restoring 'law and order'. The borders of colonial territories were generally not clearly defined, and chronic instability thus led to further and further extensions of imperial rule. The home governments often viewed these developments with great anxiety or even with extreme displeasure; but they were generally unable to curb the 'sub-imperialists' on the periphery, and in the end nearly always had to sanction the results of their actions.

However, Fieldhouse attaches much greater importance to the second form of peripheral imperialism, viz., colonial rule resulting from the collapse of the earlier form of co-operation between native élites and Europeans and the need to fill the consequent power vacuum. Fieldhouse concedes up to a point that the 'nationalist' crises on the periphery which led to the overthrow of native regimes, such as that in Egypt in 1882, and thus to a direct take-over by one or other of the European powers, were themselves due to European penetration of various kinds, but he does not accept the view that such penetration was itself imperialist. Unlike Robinson and Gallagher, whose views are in other respects close to his, Fieldhouse distinguishes fairly sharply between the older methods of informal colonialism, which were mainly economic and cultural, and dispensed with political support, and the 'new imperialism' of the period after 1880. The old colonialism was concerned first and foremost with the economic integration of the third world into the Western industrial system, without the establishment of formal political rule, whereas the 'new imperialism' after 1880 led to the establishment of direct rule on a massive scale. Fieldhouse expressly warns against attributing this later phase of European expansion to economic causes. 'Seen as an expression of the needs of the European economy, territorial imperialism becomes largely irrelevant.' It is quite possible, on the other hand, that particular economic interests that had little to do with the objective needs of the European economies exercised a 'disproportionate influence on the pattern of events' at the periphery.[54]

On the basis of this new approach, Fieldhouse maintains that it is impossible to devise a theory of imperialism which covers all possible cases and provides a once-and-for-all explanation of the extremely varied course of European expansion overseas. However, in each case the situation on the periphery constitutes a framework within which the traditional type of Eurocentric explanation gains considerably in plausibility.[55] Fieldhouse does not deny that important economic interests were at work in the process of imperialist expansion; but he stresses that it was generally economic processes on the periphery, not in the metropolis, which led the colonial powers to intervene and, in many cases, to establish direct territorial rule. He expressly denies that there was a direct link between economic motivations in the home country and territorial expansion overseas: any connection between the two is mediated by the periphery, represented either by 'men on the spot' or by the indigenous élite. Fieldhouse himself admits, however, that the establishment of more or less formal territorial or imperial rule was generally preceded by informal economic penetration; and in this respect he is quite prepared to concede that special economic interests were at work, although this tends to lessen the credibility of his general theory.

In Fieldhouse's view the extraordinary increase in the rate of expansion in the second half of the nineteenth century and the first decades of the twentieth cannot be explained primarily by intensified economic pressure, but is rather due to the crises undergone by the native societies (partly owing to informal European economic, cultural and political penetration), together with the fact that rivalries among the great powers prevented their leaving the periphery to its own devices. The 'peripheral' explanation, moreover, accounts for the fact that from the 1880s imperialism was anything but a deliberate process unfolding according to plan. It was in fact the sum of a series of largely independent *ad hoc* solutions of problems at the periphery, which acquired significance only when seen retrospectively as a whole.[56]

Fieldhouse sums up his position as follows:

The vital link between economics and formal empire was therefore neither the economic need of the metropolis for colonies nor the requirements of private economic interests, but the secondary consequence of problems created on the periphery by economic and other European enterprises for which there was no simple economic solution. At one extreme such problems directly affected what European officialdom regarded as 'first-class' national interests. At the other they raised minor political difficulties such as the instability of an indigenous political regime or obstruction by other Europeans to satisfactory trade or investment. But in virtually every case the ultimate explanation of formal annexation was that the original economic issue had to some degree become 'politicized' and therefore required a political solution.[57]

Although Fieldhouse, as we have seen, does not deny the importance of economic, political and other interests of the European industrial states, in the last resort he places the centre of gravity in the third world itself. He ascribes imperialism to two factors: firstly, the collapse of traditional political order in the overseas territories, and secondly, the natives' inability to cope with the political problems caused by European economic penetration. Despite the exculpatory effect of this theory, which is probably largely unintended, it may be regarded as important because for the first time it directs attention to the role of the indigenous population and especially its leaders, as well as that of colonial adventurers, traders, soldiers and proconsuls at the periphery. These 'sub-imperialists' were at work everywhere and often exercised a decisive influence out of all proportion to their comparatively small numbers.

Ronald Robinson, taking a more evenly balanced view, has recently related peripheral factors to a pluralistic model of imperialism, which is perhaps even more emphatic than Fieldhouse's in its rejection of traditional Eurocentrism.[58] Robinson's theory pays more attention to the actual historical course of events in each case than is usual with Eurocentric explanations; the latter, he claims, are the external projection of systems of ideas about European society rather than systematic interpretations of the processes of imperial expansion. In them, 'empire-making was conceived simply as a function of European, industrial political economy', without regard to what actually happened at the periphery; but in fact

> imperialism was a product of interaction between European and extra-European politics. European economic and strategic expansion took imperial form when these two components operated at cross-purposes with the third and non-European component—that of indigenous collaboration and resistance.[59]

Robinson starts from the premiss that the white colonialists, being extremely few in number and generally very unsure of support from the metropolis, could never have built up such great empires as they eventually did without the help of indigenous social groups. In the first phase of industrial imperialism, from about 1820 to 1870, Europeans tried to enlist the co-operation of African and Asian regimes so that these continents might be opened up to European trade and technology, without endeavouring to secure territorial dominion. In nearly all cases individuals and social groups were found at the periphery who on national grounds alone were eager for modernization and therefore prepared to co-operate with the Europeans to a considerable extent, for the most part informally. In course of time, however, this brand of imperialism undermined the collaborators' position in their own countries and often created a situation which, exacerbated by European rivalries, necessitated the establishment of direct colonial rule.

This, however, made much less difference than is usually supposed. Even after the introduction of formal European rule, the 'men on the spot' were largely obliged to work with indigenous élites, because the home governments still pursued a policy of limited commitment in terms of politics, men and money. Robinson goes so far as to say that formal imperialist rule as it was established from the 1880s onwards over large parts of the globe was often no more than a 'reconstruction of the collaboration' at the periphery which had previously collapsed owing to the upheaval of local society. Rather than follow Fieldhouse in speaking of peripheral imperialism, Robinson suggests using the concept of an 'excentric approach'.[60] He outlines a pluralistic model in which Eurocentric factors combine with peripheral ones and which, he believes, would be a profitable basis for future research. The economic dynamism of capitalism, aiming to incorporate third-world territories into the Western industrial economy, and the process of power politics whereby rival European states delimited and formalized their colonial possessions, combined with the internal processes of native societies to bring about imperial expansion. In this development, Robinson unhesitatingly lays the main emphasis on the periphery. True, the manifestations of crisis at the periphery were due in part to informal European influence and free-trade imperialism, but they also sprang from independent local causes; and it was they which first induced the European powers to switch from informal control to formal rule on the European model. In most cases the statesmen concerned were by no means pleased at this development, nor were they inclined to set the new colonial administrations on a really firm foundation. In other words, imperialism was not a rational, deliberate, well-planned enterprise but a highly complex process which both its European agents and their victims regarded as accidental but inevitable, and which increasingly escaped their control.

Any modern theory of imperialism must face the challenge of the 'peripheral school'. This school appears at first sight to be largely a defensive exercise, at least in the cases of Fieldhouse and Platt; but it has certainly set the problem in an entirely new light and contains elements which make it possible to assess, more precisely than with any of the previous theories, the long-term effects of imperialism on the world of today and on relations between the industrial states and the underdeveloped countries. One of the most noteworthy aspects of the peripheral approach is certainly the importance it attaches to the part played by indigenous 'collaborators' in determining the objectives and timing of imperial annexation. Secondly it brings to light a point hitherto insufficiently emphasized, that European imperialists often found it the easiest solution of their problems to maintain native collaborationist regimes in power even after the latter had lost the support of their countrymen. In the short term this limited formal imperialist expansion, but it often had a decisive effect in preventing the political and social modernization of the indigenous society. In such cases the groups which mistrusted formal imperial expansion and saw it as, at best, an unavoidable necessity were most often those who preferred the strategy of indirect control to formal colonial rule. In this way European imperialism had a retarding effect on the political development of the third world and its progress towards maturity in many spheres. The ultimate consequences of this process are a major factor in the present world situation.

five

Theories of Neo-Colonialism and Underdevelopment

1 Imperialism as state monopoly capitalism

Contrary to the predictions of Lenin and Rosa Luxemburg, the disappearance of formal colonial rule—a process which began in 1919 and was precipitately completed after the Second World War—left the Western capitalist system essentially unscathed. Evidently capitalism was able to overcome its inner contradictions without the aid of imperialist structures in the third world, at any rate those of a formal character. True, in regard to certain raw materials, the West is still considerably dependent on third-world countries, especially those of the Middle East, as was shown dramatically by the 'oil crisis' of 1974. But that crisis also showed that the Western powers are no longer in a position to use political, let alone military, power to protect their economic interests in third-world countries. From this point of view, at least, the age of imperialism is dead and buried.

However, Western theorists have been somewhat premature in concluding that, with the advent of decolonization and democratic self-determination, at least in the Western industrial states, imperialism is in principle a thing of the past, its last survivals having virtually disappeared since Spain and Portugal gave up their overseas possessions. The question must still be answered, whether the grant of formal independence to ex-colonial territories has really put an end to imperialism, or whether the after-effects of imperial rule have not persisted in spite of decolonization. Meanwhile Marxist-Leninists, for their part, have been obliged to modify their own basic position, even though to a large extent it enjoyed the status of a canonized body of truth. This is especially the case with neo-Marxist theorists in Western countries, who are not, like their colleagues in the Eastern bloc, sheltered from serious criticism thanks to official manipulation of public opinion. While in the Eastern countries it still appears possible to go on repeating in wholesale fashion the old formulae about the imperialist nature of capitalism,[1] in the West there has for some time been a lively debate in progress about the interrelation of the two ideas—though the argument is admittedly highly diffuse and is not easy to reduce to precise terms.

To begin with there is a large group of neo-Marxists who, while differing on specific points, are concerned to reformulate Marxist-Leninist theory in the light of the actual development of the capitalist world system and thus restore its political cutting edge—an objective which often leads to a blurring of the distinction between critical theory and political agitation. The members of this group are agreed in holding that capitalism in its more recent development has evolved a number of devices which to some extent make colonial rule unnecessary, as they neutralize by other means the law of falling profits and the increasingly acute inner contradictions of the capitalist system of production. Imperialism, at any rate in the sense of the domination and economic exploitation of undeveloped peripheral territories, no longer appears necessary to the maintenance of the capitalist system, but is seen by these critics merely as a consistent strategic device of monopoly capitalism under 'late capitalist' conditions.

Maurice Dobb and Paul Sweezy, in particular, wrote in the 1930s of 'state monopoly capitalism' as a qualitatively new phase of development characterized by increasing state intervention in the economic process.[2] As Dobb put it in his *Studies in the Development of Capitalism*: 'The common element in these various species is the coexistence of capitalist ownership and operation of production with a system of generalized controls over economic operation exercised by the State, which pursues ends that are not identical with those of an individual firm.'[3] Engels's conception of the state as an 'ideal collective capitalist' is systematically developed by Sweezy and Dobb, who also give it a specific political slant. It is the interventionist state—though this concept is not yet actually formulated—which ensures the continuation of the capitalist system by measures directed in the first instance at the internal market. On the one hand a militarist policy turns the state itself into a producer of purchasing power, continually syphoning off a considerable part of surplus production in the form of unproductive expenditure on armaments, and thus of course greatly increasing the risk of war. On the other hand the state is able, by intervening in the business cycle, to mitigate the harmful effects of economic crises, and to take measures in the field of social policy which prevent a dangerous exacerbation of social tension. By means of state contracts and by enlarging the state-controlled sector of the economy it was possible to create a substitute for the function of imperialist capital exports, which had already begun to lose their importance in the 1920s because of the awakening of national resistance in the third world. In this connection Dobb and Sweezy interpret Nazism and Fascism as an attempt to open up new possibilities of capital expansion in Europe instead of overseas. In conditions of state monopoly capitalism, imperialism takes on a new colour: it becomes a contest among the industrial states for the control and economic exploitation of comparatively well developed parts of the world, the penetration of peripheral areas having lost much of its importance. But decolonization no longer presents an acute danger to capitalism, as the state monopoly system is capable of providing other correctives and palliatives, albeit at the cost of continual external conflicts and some internal ones also.

The studies of modern imperialism by George William F. Hallgarten are in many ways close to the views of Dobb and Sweezy, though they are far more systematically worked out as far as economic causes are concerned. His most important work is *Imperialismus vor 1914*,[4] written in the early 1930s, to which Hallgarten added, shortly before his death, a supplement bringing the story to the present day and entitled 'The Fate of

Imperialism in the Twentieth Century'.[5] Hallgarten's approach is primarily socio-Marxist, based on an analysis of the interactions of leading groups[6] which, it must be said, does not reach the theoretical level of original Marxism, arguing as it does from considerations of individual psychology. Arguing from such premises he was at pains to identify and pillory the wire-pullers in the world of industry and finance capital who were responsible for the imperialist actions of the great powers, especially Britain and Germany; few of his specific conclusions, however, are really convincing. Following Lenin, Hallgarten does not confine the notion of imperialism to territorial annexation and economic exploitation of underdeveloped areas, but regards it as a direct expression of the internal structure of the capitalist system. On this basis he describes imperialism as follows:

Imperialism and capitalism together signify war against workers at home and natives in the colonies. This is the world of monopolies, bank capital and trusts, in arms against the rest of mankind; and it finally embraces the totality of the white population, brought into action by these forces. Spurred by the surplus of industrial goods and the scarcity of raw materials in European countries, imperialism propels these countries into various adventures. In order to embark on its world-wide course it mobilizes and makes use of a huge army of volunteers and auxiliaries, including thousands of financial and commercial agents, military instructors, doctors, engineers, geographers, geologists, other political and industrial specialists, teachers and even missionaries. The target and the victims of all this activity comprise all countries which are less developed economically than the capitalist powers of Europe. These include certain large, backward, economically underdeveloped countries like Tsarist Russia; young countries that have not yet been opened up economically, like the Balkan and Latin American states in their time; the old oriental monarchies, like Japan, China, Turkey and Persia; victims of the mercantilist colonialism of former centuries, like India; and the inhabitants of colonies in Asia, Africa and the Pacific, acquired during the period of imperialism. It can be seen that the victims of imperialism were numbered among all races of the earth, including the white race.[7]

According to Hallgarten, heavy industry and high finance were the chief motive forces of world politics in the last few decades before 1914. He also held that heavy industry bore the main blame for Hitler's accession to power in 1933, fascism in general being a special variant of imperialism.

Hallgarten distinguished three phases of imperialism: the first coinciding with the classic period of imperialism down to 1918, the second from then till 1945, and the third characterized by the rivalry of the two present-day superpowers. During the second phase the major industrial powers were largely dependent on the decisions of one or two charismatic leaders, and, in consequence, 'the distinguishing feature of imperialism in the second stage is that the masses were directly involved in it'.[8] He acknowledges, however, in opposition to classic Marxism-Leninism, that monopoly capitalism today no longer has to rely on colonies in the strict sense, as their function has been taken over by armaments. His severest criticism is naturally directed at the United States, which, as the most highly developed capitalist society in history, is compared with the slave-based economy of ancient Rome. U.S. armaments, apart from creating a maximum of politico-strategic security, are devoted to stabilizing capitalism and spreading it throughout the world.[9] Despite these interpretations of imperialism, which in general suggest a global politico-economic view, in his analyses of specific imperialist phenomena Hallgarten adheres to an individualistic variant of Marxism which fastens attention not on the expansive tendencies of capitalism as such but on the sinister economic interests of particular entrepreneurs or bankers and their personal connections with those in power. Imperialism is here depicted as a permanent conspiracy of high finance and heavy industry, but not as a process due to the economic structure as such. To this extent Hallgarten's unconscious reasoning still remains within the framework of the classic liberalist conception of the capitalist economy which he has, so to speak, merely stood on its head.

2 Imperialism as the rule of big monopolies

A development of the Marxist position, looking back to the older theory of monopoly capitalism and extending it to multinational corporations, can be found in the work of authors such as Tom Kemp.[10] Kemp argues that, although Lenin's predictions about the future of the capitalist system have not been entirely fulfilled, his theory of monopoly capitalism is still valid and provides by far the best key to the interpretation of present capitalist tendencies. The distinctive feature of Kemp's position, in which he is fully representative of recent developments in the neo-Marxist camp, is that he no longer assigns to the political system a relatively independent role within the socio-political process. In this respect he differs from Sweezy and Dobb, and especially Hallgarten, who were all directly influenced by the phenomenon of fascism and the fact that it was not manifestly due to economic causes alone. Other authors, such as Ernest Mandel, have in the main followed Kemp's line in this respect.[11] Kemp rightly points out that Lenin's theory of imperialism 'put the emphasis on the structural changes in capitalism rather than upon the relations between the metropolitan countries and their colonies', and argues that it is still fruitful for this very reason.[12]

This partial return to orthodoxy suggests a new departure within the neo-Marxist debate, viz., the shifting of the argument towards the activities of the big monopolies and multinational companies. It is they, and not the state as an 'ideal collective capitalist', who are now presented as the real exponents of imperialism: state power is increasingly dependent on economic decisions by the great corporations, and traditional forms of political domination on the basis of independent nation states are increasingly obsolete. In Kemp's view the situation at the present day is above all determined by the increasingly firm hold of big corporations over the state.

> The intimate relations established between the big private corporations, including those of a 'multinational' character, and the state make it increasingly difficult to tell where the sphere of private capital ends. The state is drawn directly into the arena, not merely to defend the general legal conditions for private ownership and commodity production but also actively to assist the process of accumulation.[13]

On these premisses Kemp interprets imperialism, in the world situation of today, as signifying primarily informal economic rule by international and finance-capitalist corporations, based especially on the United States. The analysis of the capitalist system in the circumstances of decolonization thus turns into a theory of underdevelopment as being, so to speak, the reverse side of the rule of monopoly capitalism—precarious, but still unbroken—over the most important economic resources of the globe.

With some differences of emphasis this may serve as a description of the most recent development of neo-Marxist theory in general. The argument which has been widely adopted is that decolonization has meant only a change in the tactics of capitalism and not in its strategy. The continuing economic dependence of the developing countries on the industrial states is only an expression of the contradictions still inherent in the capitalist system. The present economic conflicts between industrial and developing countries, and the fact that the gap between them is at present widening rather than narrowing, are regarded by these neo-Marxist authors as a proof of the basic accuracy of Marxist theory; analysis of the concrete phenomena of economic backwardness is much less in evidence, although it is becoming increasingly prominent in the latest Marxist works on imperialism.

It is true in general of these variants of the neo-Marxist theory of imperialism, as Kemp candidly says of his own, that it is intended to be more than simply a 'tool for understanding the course of world development' as it proceeds, directly or indirectly, from the era of classic imperialism: it is intended to 'raise the political consciousness of the working class' and bring about the revolutionary transformation of the world.[14]

At the same time there are occasional attempts to break free from the dogmatism of Lenin's theory of imperialism and to find a starting-point for the formulation of a new theory by returning to Marx himself. The results of this movement have not been highly impressive. Christel Neusüss, for instance, formulates the thesis, which will probably hardly stand comparison with the empirical data, that the internationalization of capital, i.e., the imperialist expansion of the Western industrial states, took place in three stages: a first stage of commercial exchange, a second one of capital export, and finally the present stage of economic control by multinational concerns. The aid of the national state, however, was, she contends, only sought when this process was threatened with reversal.[15]

Another shift of emphasis is found in the work of Harry Magdoff.[16] Magdoff conforms to the traditional Marxist-Leninist model in so far as he regards imperialism as a necessary stage of capitalism and in particular (as Lenin held) capitalism in its monopoly phase. But he rejects certain basic features of traditional Marxist theory, particularly the thesis that when opportunities of colonial exploitation are exhausted it will mean the collapse of capitalism. Magdoff also disclaims the view that imperialist expansion is caused by an excessive supply of surplus capital and that overseas investments are sought in order to evade the law of falling rates of profit. With regard to the most recent development, marked by general reluctance to invest in third-world countries, Magdoff produces other explanatory models combining economic and political factors. The decisive feature, he says, is the mutual rivalry of great monopolies in the metropolitan countries, the effect of which is that all possibilities of expansion tend to be exhausted, whether with political support or not. Magdoff points out that economic expansion, together with a steady enlargement of the field of investment, is an essential feature of capitalist development in conditions of monopoly capitalism, and that it was intensified by the existence of several highly industrialized states in competition with one another. He also refers to the close correlation between capitalist societies and nationalist structures.

> The nationalism of capitalist societies is the *alter ego* of the system's internationalism. Successful capitalist classes need the power of nation states not only to develop inner markets and to build adequate infrastructures but also, and equally important, to secure and protect opportunities for foreign commerce and investment in a world of rival nation states.[17]

Magdoff concedes that governments are not simply subject to pressure by interested business circles, but depend on the class or classes to which they owe their power in general. At the same time all governments, or at any rate those which practise foresight, are more or less obliged to pursue a policy favourable to the development of capitalism and all its potentialities, including the safeguarding by imperialist means of the nation's economic chances, or rather those of its capitalist class. The political factor is only one among many, and consequently the end of colonialism by no means signifies the end of imperialism. Rather, in Magdoff's view, the mechanisms of a mature industrial society, and in particular the interests of big monopolies and multinational concerns, tend to perpetuate to the maximum extent the economic and financial dependence of third-world countries on the metropolitan states. Only the presence of the USSR has to some extent offset the working of these mechanisms.

Magdoff's interpretation is thus summed up in the thesis that imperialism signifies economic rule by the big monopolies (despite their mutual rivalry), either exercised by simple pre-eminence or in the form of overt colonialism. Imperialism continues after colonialism has formally come to an end. The colonial period served only to adapt the social and economic institutions of the dependent countries to metropolitan needs. Once this was done, the colonial relationship persisted after the establishment of formal political independence, thanks to the informal economic, financial and social structures that had been created. For the socio-economic structure of these countries then guaranteed that the forms of colonial domination that had prevailed in the past would 'reproduce' themselves indefinitely without the need of further political action by the ex-metropolis.

It is not a simple matter to eradicate dependency relations that have ripened and become embedded over a long stretch of history, beginning with the days of mercantilism. In the several developmental stages of the trade and financial ties of the colonial and semi-colonial economies, the economic structure of the latter became increasingly adapted to its [*sic*] role as an appendage of the metropolitan centre. The composition of prices, the income distribution and the allocation of resources evolved, with the aid of military power as well as the blind forces of the market, in such a way as continuously to reproduce the dependency.[18]

✳(These arguments are close to the views of those theorists who see a direct connection between the 'vicious circle of underdevelopment' and imperialism, and who assert that the true mark of imperialism is that it perpetuates and increases the poverty of the developing countries in order that capital may accumulate more and more rapidly in the industrial states) We shall now turn to an examination of these theories.

3 Underdevelopment as a product of imperialism

The revival of the Leninist concept of monopoly capitalism, which is a general feature of the most recent neo-Marxist literature, is a key to the modern Marxist theory of neo-colonialism and underdevelopment, which can be regarded as an ideological counterpart to Western theories of modernization. From this point of view imperialism is equated with the control of big monopolies, including of course the multinational corporations, over the underdeveloped regions of the earth. To these theorists it is of secondary importance whether the monopolies make use of state power to assert their interests at the periphery, or whether they rely chiefly on the informal but effective weapon of their disproportionate economic superiority. They lay great stress on the view, which they often put forward as though it were self-evident, that the third world has been exploited no less thoroughly by monopoly capitalism since the colonial empires ceased to exist, although it is sometimes conceded that the imperialist forces are now on the defensive.

The political origins of this theory are unmistakable. Not only official Soviet policy but, as we have seen,[19] many of the Afro-Asian countries have all along contended that the economic links with former colonies which survived the grant of formal political independence, and also the system of 'development aid', merely represented new forms of imperialist bondage, effected primarily by informal means. Kwame Nkrumah described this by the succinct formula of 'neo-colonialism, the last stage of capitalism'. Neo-colonialism, in his view, signified the indirect exploitation of underdeveloped peoples by means of 'unequal' trade relations, the export of capital on terms unfavourable to the receiver country, artificial manipulation of the terms of trade, and finally development aid. An important part was played by formally independent puppet governments at the periphery, acting in the interests of the white capitalists: only with their help could imperialism maintain its control over those areas. Nkrumah described neo-colonialism as the worst form of imperialism, inasmuch as it allowed absolutely no defence against corrupt mismanagement by collaborationist regimes in the third world.

> For those who practise it, it means power without responsibility, and for those who suffer from it, it means exploitation without redress. In the days of old-fashioned colonialism, the imperial power had at least to explain and justify at home the actions it was taking abroad. In the colony those who served the ruling imperial power could at least look to

its protection against any violent move by their opponents. With neo-colonialism neither is the case.[20]

In other words, the socio-economic structures that had formed during the period of imperialism remained unimpaired after the end of formal colonial rule, and were moreover now exempt from any kind of political supervision, and the same was true of one-sided economic relations designed for the benefit of the former colonial ruler. In addition, Nkrumah complained that foreign business interests were not interested in the modernization of third-world countries but, on the contrary, endeavoured to prevent their economic and technological development.

In the 1950s Nkrumah was probably the most conspicuous third-world leader to criticize 'neo-colonialism' from a neo-Marxist point of view, but he was by no means the only one. His views were echoed by numerous Afro-Marxists and sympathizers in the West: they recur with tedious uniformity, though with varying degrees of emphasis, throughout neo-Marxist literature on the subject of underdevelopment. A distinction must, however, be drawn between theorists who emphasize the socio-psychological consequences of imperialism, and the permanent distortion of the psychic structure of ex-colonial peoples which is said to result from it, and, on the other hand, the main body of neo-Marxist writers who maintain that underdevelopment in the third world is directly or indirectly due to imperialism and the continuing relationship of dependence between the colonies and their former owners.

A typical exposition of the first view is Frantz Fanon's

The Wretched of the Earth. [21] Fanon spoke of the profound psychic damage done by imperialism to the former colonial peoples and especially their leaders, preventing their complete emancipation from white tutelage. Drawing his examples from French colonial history, he showed how difficult it was for these peoples to recover a national identity of their own after the formal termination of colonial rule. To remedy this state of affairs, Fanon advocated a violent revolt by the ex-colonials in order to create a new national culture, destroying at a blow the invisible fetters of centuries of spiritual and cultural 'self-alienation'. As Fanon puts it: 'The conscious and organized undertaking by a colonized people to re-establish the sovereignty of that nation constitutes the most complete and obvious cultural manifestation that exists.' He recognizes that the fight for national liberation cannot bring about the simple restoration of the pre-imperial national culture; but its value is that it prepares the way for the creation of a new national consciousness that is nevertheless in line with the old tradition. 'The struggle for freedom does not give back to the national culture its former value and shapes; this struggle, which aims at a fundamentally different set of relations between men, cannot leave intact either the form or the content of the people's culture.' [22] But even under such conditions, which are the most favourable from the standpoint of creating truly independent Afro-Asian national states, grave psychological damage will have been done to the colonial peoples and especially their leading groups, so that complete emancipation from the European model is a matter of great difficulty. In this way, Fanon argues, the imperialism of the past throws a shadow over the future of the young nations of the third world even long after the end of formal colonialism.

As regards the economic effect of imperialism, many Marxist authors in the West argue with still greater emphasis that imperialist rule has continued since the end of formal colonialism, which has scarcely affected economic structures as such. For instance, Paul A. Baran's *The Political Economy of Growth*, first published in 1957,[23] argued forcefully that the exploitation of the third world had continued unabated since the termination of colonial rule, at a new level and with far greater efficiency.

> The contemporary form of imperialism . . . is now directed not solely towards the rapid extraction of large sporadic gains from the objects of its domination, it is no longer content with merely assuring a more or less steady flow of those gains over a somewhat extended period. Propelled by well-organized, rationally conducted monopolistic enterprise, it seeks today to rationalize the flow of these receipts so as to be able to count on it in perpetuity.[24]

In other words, according to Baran, the underdeveloped countries are more than ever enslaved to the interests of monopoly capital. This basic fact has scarcely been affected by the end of formal colonial rule in the third world, as all the territories concerned have fallen under 'comprador governments' which make common cause with foreign capital. 'The exploitation of raw materials in undeveloped countries by foreign capital, and the existence of wasteful, corrupt and reactionary comprador regimes in these countries, are not fortuitous coincidences but merely different if closely intercon-

nected aspects of what can only be adequately understood as the totality of imperialism.'[25] Baran thus argues
that socio-economic structures which have taken shape
at the periphery provide a lasting basis for the interests
of monopoly capital based on the metropolis, even after
the grant of formal independence. 'Under such conditions the political independence barely won turns into a
sham, the new ruling group merges with the old ruling
group, and the amalgam of property-owning classes supported by imperialist interests uses its entire power to
suppress the popular movement for genuine national
and social liberation.'[26]

In Baran's view, continued imperialist dependence
after the end of the colonial period is ensured first and
foremost by the reproduction of socio-economic and political structures at the periphery in accordance with the
interests of the metropolitan powers. This is the main
cause of the chronic economic backwardness of the developing countries, since the overriding interest of European monopoly capitalism is 'to prevent, or, if that is
impossible, to slow down and to control the economic
development of undeveloped countries'.[27] As Baran un-
compromisingly puts it, the irrationality of the present
system 'will not be overcome so long as its basis, the
capitalist system, continues to exist'.[28]

The contrast between the increasing impoverishment
of the developing countries and the capital accumulation
by industrial monopolists is emphasized even more
strongly by authors such as André Gunder Frank, who
writes chiefly on Latin America, and Pierre Jalée, A.
Emmanuel, Samir Amin and Christian Palloix, whose
arguments are drawn mainly from the experience of for-

mer French colonies. André G. Frank defines imperialism in a very wide sense as the decisive final phase of the economic penetration of third-world countries in the interest of monopoly capital in the metropolitan states, especially the United States. This is not merely a matter of the peaceful penetration of the local economy by means of increasing capital investment: its ultimate purpose is to bind the country's economic and political institutions to the capitalist system, and in this it is often helped by native governments and the native bourgeoisie. In the case of Latin America, 'neo-imperialism and monopoly capitalist development are drawing and driving the entire bourgeois class . . . into ever closer economic and political alliance with, and dependence on, the imperialist metropolis', i.e., in this case the United States.[29]

This analysis is, of course, based on the assumption, which implies a rosy view of pre-imperial conditions, that Latin America could have modernized itself but for the interference of foreign monopoly capital. It also involves the accusation that monopoly capitalism is not only perpetuating but systematically aggravating the backwardness of Latin America by its use of capital investment and by building up huge monopolies so as to exploit the area's raw materials for the benefit of the metropolitan country. By one-sided emphasis on raw material production based on the development of monocultures, and by the constant syphoning off of net profits from its own investments, capitalism has prevented the Latin American countries from developing an independent economy of their own and has thus made certain that the broad masses will become poorer and poorer. In other words, the imperialist system, which in Latin America signifies nothing more nor less than economic domination by foreign and especially U.S. concerns, does not tend to produce modernization but, on the contrary, 'structural underdevelopment'.[30] According to Frank the only way of escape from this vicious circle of under-development is a socialist revolution, and it is the duty of all Latin American intellectuals to work for this.[31]

Indisputably these theories denouncing a system in which the rich constantly get richer and the poor poorer display considerable moral persuasiveness. But there is room for a difference of opinion as to their validity, firstly because they are based on an idealization of pre-imperialist conditions which cannot be taken seriously, and above all because they do not in the end get any further than a general arraignment of capitalism. For instance, André G. Frank's definition of imperialism is really tautological. He uses the term to signify no more and no less than the international capitalist system itself: the formation of capitalist economic systems at the periphery is in itself 'imperialistic', though it is an aggravating circumstance if they serve the interests of the capitalist metropolis. The internationalization of capital invested in Latin America is in itself inadequate evidence of the allegedly imperialist or neo-colonialist character of the Latin American economy, especially as it is only true to a very limited extent that there has been direct political support of informal economic penetration by European and subsequently U.S. capital. And the lack of such evidence is not compensated for by incessantly repeating that foreign capitalist interests have deliberately prevented the modernization of Latin American states.

A. Emmanuel, Pierre Jalée, Samir Amin and other theorists of the 'dependence' school have endeavoured to prove specifically that the inherent structure of the capitalist world system is opposed to the modernization of the third world and inevitably tends to increase its backwardness. Two themes are given prominence here: firstly that of 'unfair trading', i.e., the fixing of unfair prices for goods exported by the industrial and the developing countries respectively, and secondly the role of multinational concerns with their uncontrollable influence in the markets of the third world especially. Thus Emmanuel has argued that the shift of the terms of trade against the developing countries is not only an effect of the international system which places raw material exporting countries at a disadvantage *vis-à-vis* those that mainly export industrial goods, but that it is also due to manipulation by international organizations in favour of the metropolitan countries.[32]

Jalée for his part asserts that a significant feature of the 'latest stage of imperialism' is the 'complete subordination of the third world economy to that of the imperialist system'.[33] This subordination is achieved by three principal means. Firstly, by huge private capital investments, which make it possible to syphon off a large surplus in the third world; secondly, by public 'development aid', which ensures the continuance of this one-sided system by closing the gap in the chronic balance-of-payments deficit of the underdeveloped countries; and thirdly, by the influence of social groups at the periphery whose interest links them to the capitalist world system.[34] Palloix[35] in particular points out, moreover, that a system of international division of labour leads to a reallocation of industries to the detriment of the developing countries.

While the industrial countries concentrate on industries with a future, the developing countries are left with branches of production at a lower technological level and with less prospect of growth—a situation which must tend to perpetuate the economic gap between them. In accordance with this aspect of the 'dependence' theory, Samir Amin and Dieter Senghaas have recently outlined a 'theory of peripheral capitalism' which may be regarded as a modern variant of the classic theory of imperialism. In many ways this follows lines of interpretation which were formulated by Rosa Luxemburg but which she did not develop consistently. Amin and Senghaas start from the premiss that underdevelopment in the third world is due to the fact that what happened at the periphery was as a rule *not* a complete triumph of modern imperialism but only a partial involvement of the local economies in the world system, which prevented the formation of an independent industrial structure capable of 'autocentric' development. This form of integration in the international system is marked by a high degree of specialization corresponding to the needs of the metropolis rather than to those of the under-developed country in question. Despite their formal political independence, the third-world countries are drawn willy-nilly into a system of international division of labour which consistently favours the dominant centres and disfavours the dependent, dominated peripheral countries.[36] This is the direct consequence of the forced integration of the third-world economies with those of the metropolis, which took place in colonial and imperial times, and the related policy of establishing metropolitan bridgeheads in the peripheral countries. Furthermore, the imperialists' policy of 'divide and conquer' worked against the possibility of the third-world countries combining to resist these tendencies. The cultural, political and especially economic structures which had been imposed on them prevented their developing an independent economy corresponding to the needs of all sections of their population. The asymmetrical integration of the third-world countries into the international capitalist system stood in the way of an 'autocentric development' such as most European countries had achieved after being initially dependent on the pioneer industrial states. As Senghaas argues,

> such autocentric development, bearing in itself its own capacity of reproduction, is something which cannot be attained by dependent socio-economic entities, whose integration in the capitalist world system on a division-of-labour basis has afflicted them with a dependent and deformed system of reproduction (monoculture, outward orientation of the dynamic sectors of the economy, marginalization, etc.).[37]

According to this school of thought, peripheral capitalism, being governed entirely by external interests, is characterized by the coexistence of pre-industrial forms of reproduction on the one hand and, on the other, industries that are technologically advanced but confined to specialized sectors: in other words, bridgeheads of great wealth amid extreme, continuing poverty on a vast scale. This state of affairs must be regarded as the logical result of imperialist penetration in bygone ages. Even after the political rule of the metropolitan countries was over, the informal means of control established during the period of economic penetration of the dependent countries continued to operate; the socio-economic structures created by them made it impossible to alter this dependency, and thus perpetuated the under-development of the peripheral countries.

The theories here discussed vary in the importance they attach to the different factors which, it is claimed, tend to perpetuate the relationship of dependency even after the end of formal imperial rule. Baran emphasizes the reproduction of the socio-economic structures of the capitalist metropolis at the periphery; Emmanuel, Jalée and Baran see the decisive factor in the asymmetrical economic relations between third-world countries and the advanced industrial states; Amin and Senghaas emphasize the structural obstacles to the development of dynamic industrial systems corresponding to local needs. All these critics agree, however, in holding that these structures of 'dependency' are essentially due to the inherent mechanism of the international capitalist system, which is such that political rule in the narrower sense is no longer an essential pre-requisite of imperialist domination, once the capitalist system has been firmly established at the periphery and stabilized by close economic links between the metropolis and native ruling circles. In such circumstances political means of coercion can be largely dispensed with. Instead, the universal phenomenon is 'dependent reproduction on the basis of structural violence'.[38] These arguments are complemented by reference to the growing power of multinational corporations, which by a skilful combination of policies—capital investment, price-fixing and production based on the world-wide division of labour—are in a position largely to control the economies of the third-world countries. As Jalée and O'Connor (and also Magdoff) have argued, the development of new monopoly capital organizations of this type, mostly with their base in the United States, has led to the creation of a new kind of 'super-imperialism', paralleled by the formation of a new 'international class'.[39]

It is doubtful, however, whether this line of thought is any longer useful as an effective research strategy, or whether it leads to much more than a body of tautologous statements about the functioning of the capitalist system as such. According to these theories themselves, those who exercise imperial rule have become anonymous entities and can no longer be brought to book. O'Connor, for instance, defines 'economic imperialism' as 'the economic control of one country or territory over another; specifically, formal or informal control over indigenous economic resources in a way advantageous to the metropolis and at the expense of the satellites' own economy'.[40] But what does this mean when the multinational companies on which this argument fastens its attention are steadily losing their national character, so that it is no longer meaningful to talk of one country dominating another by economic means? Moreover, one is justified in asking whether the activity of multinational corporations is in practice always detrimental to third-world countries.[41] The trouble with the present situation is rather, on the contrary, that international capital is increasingly neglecting these countries and thus giving them less chance than ever to draw even with the big industrial states. A switch-over to a socialist mode of production would not basically affect the disparity in economic potential between the industrial and the developing countries; hence some more concrete solution must be found for the dilemma of underdevelopment, especially as existing socialist societies have shown that they are no less skilled than their Western rivals in the technique of formal or informal imperialist exploitation.

4 Imperialism as dependence based on 'structural violence'

Developing these neo-Marxist interpretations, but in addition treating the socialist states as both subjects and objects of 'super-imperialism', Johan Galtung has recently made a noteworthy attempt to develop a formal theory of imperialism which largely ignores its actual historical manifestations and defines it as a 'special type of domination by one organized community over another'.[42] Galtung looks back to the ideas of the 'peripheral school' and describes imperialist rule as a form of structural dependence that originates between a 'central' and a 'peripheral' nation as the result of a complicated mechanism, the chief feature of which is that the centre possesses a bridgehead on the periphery in the form of a co-operative indigenous ruling class whose values are very similar to those of the metropolis, and which has an interest in the preservation of the existing order. Imperialist dependence is thus essentially due to a difference in the degree of social inequality, which is greater at the periphery than in the metropolis and operates to the latter's benefit. Lenin's idea of the aristocracy of the working class being bribed with the surplus profits of imperialism is here applied to conditions at the periphery.

On this theory the feudal interaction, dating from colonial times, between the 'peripheral' and the 'central' nation strengthens the tendency towards an asymmetrical trade structure, which already exists because the periphery generally figures on the international market as an exporter of raw materials. But above all this feudal relationship offers a decisive advantage to the élites which can deal direct with the central nation. There thus arises a form of 'structural dependence' which, if it is complete, no longer requires political and military support. 'Only imperfect imperialism has need of armed force; professional imperialism relies on structural violence rather than direct coercion.'[43]

Arguing in a formalized way, Galtung concludes that imperialist rule is based on a reproduction of more or less authoritarian patterns of domination at the periphery, as compared with relatively democratic structures in the central nation itself. It may be questioned how far this interpretation fits the actual course of events in Europe or the third world, since we find that on the periphery the process of emancipation from colonial rule goes hand in hand with the establishment of 'development dictatorships', in the creation of which the central nations have no part.

This model of imperialist dependence based on asymmetrical relations is differentiated by Galtung from the viewpoint of present conditions, on the one hand by distinguishing five types of imperialism—economic, political, military, cultural and 'communications imperialism'—and on the other by refining the pattern of dependence, so that intermediary nations come into play between the centre and the periphery: the model thus takes on a multinational aspect, though this too does not necessarily improve its practical applicability. France or West Germany, for instance, may function in some parts of the world as intermediaries for the central imperialist nation which is the United States. This construction is problematical not only by reason of its highly abstract character but above all because of the assumptions it involves concerning the practical mechanism of dependence. Thus Galtung asserts with some boldness that the international organizations have today become no more than instruments of the 'asymmetrical interaction' between central and peripheral nations which was in the past assured by formal colonial rule. To judge from the United Nations, the case at present is, on the contrary, that the West is circumscribed by a third-world majority in the international forum. Doubt is also aroused as to the validity of Galtung's thesis that the 'spin-off effects' generated by asymmetrical interaction structures must in all cases favour the industrial nations. Recent developments concerning the production of raw materials, especially oil, have shown that the contrary may well be the case. At all events, it can no longer be said that the West, by means of 'structural violence', is in all circumstances able to impose unfavourable terms of trade on the third world.

Critique → Theories of the type described here suffer from the fact that they largely ignore the historical manifestations of imperialism and are in danger of becoming mere empty formulae of a purely ideological nature. Any change in the actual structure of the world economy at the present time may, as we have seen, deprive them of much of their probative force. Nevertheless they deserve our attention, since they are addressed to one of the sorest points of the present-day international order, viz. the relation of the industrial countries to the third world.) Those who propound them are concerned to discover the reason why large parts of the globe are still backward despite the universal triumph of the modern industrial system. They have helped to disturb our complacent assurance that, given time, the inherent dynamics of Western industrialism will bring the third-world countries into the Western camp, an assumption which has hitherto been accepted rather unthinkingly by Marxists, liberals and conservatives alike. To this extent the theorists of underdevelopment may help us to solve the burning question of how to close the widening gap between rich and poor nations—if only by compelling the Western world to face the problems that arise, instead of relying on the supposed self-regulating force of the international economic system, or resigning itself to what is frequently assumed to be without remedy.

six

Summary and Prospects

The foregoing survey of modern theories of imperialism since their beginnings in the late nineteenth century has presented a multiplicity of views, all based on specific political attitudes yet all, in different degrees, contributing to an understanding of the subject. In some cases they can easily be combined with one another and thus lead to a more critical analysis of imperialist phenomena, but in many others they seem incompatible and irreconcilable. Despite the changes in our attitude towards the imperialist age now that the classic type of formal imperialism has become a thing of the past, a remarkable degree of continuity can be seen in both bourgeois and Marxist studies of the subject. The broad lines of a possible interpretation of imperialism or imperialisms were already laid down by such classic theorists as Hobson, Hilferding, Schumpeter and Lenin; later writers have endeavoured, on the basis of these studies, to produce more differentiated models taking into account recent